Family Love Letters

A Treasure Chest of Memories

Praise for
Family Love Letters

In Family Love Letters, *Bob has created a jewel with the treasures (letters) from family members that he and his wife, Diane, collected and kept over the years. It has amazed me that he saved them from so many years. From these letters, he wove together memories recalled in a loving, real-life, and humorous way that makes the book so interesting to read. I recommend this book to you.*

- Ron Cook, Minster of Pastoral Care, King Street Church

Family Love Letters *is a natural sequel to* Average Man, Almighty Companion. *We now learn more about Bob's path to Christianity through actual letters written by beloved family members. If you are of a certain age, this book will likely bring back memories of your grandparents and a slower paced world. This book illustrates how God's Upper story unfolds over time through Bob's wonderful treasure chest of memories.*

- Rick Alexander, Operations Manager, Alpha Media

The art of letter writing has been lost on today's society. In this book, the letters the author discovers are a priceless link to his past. However, more important even than that are the letters from God in this book that will link you to your future.

- Paul Stutzman, author of Hiking Through

As a boy growing up in southern Pennsylvania in the spring I would go outside and play without shoes. It would hurt my feet until they toughened up, but once that happened, I could even run over stones without it hurting. As I read Bob's book I was reminded of those times. Through sharing his stories of letters, Bob gives many insights into growing up and how tough that was. As you read this book, pay close attention to how Bob's life was shaped. Family, love, joy and above all Jesus made the difference. From a soul that was lost, to one that was found, Bob does a masterful job in his story of showing how one can come to that same place of peace that he found.

- Pastor Glenn D. Peck

Family Love Letters

A Treasure Chest of Memories

ROBERT JONES

Copyright
Robert Jones, Chambersburg, PA
Copyright © Robert Jones, 2021
All rights reserved. No part of this book may be reproduced in any form without permission in writing from the author. Reviewers may quote brief passages in reviews.2020

DISCLAIMER
No part of this publication may be reproduced or transmitted in any form or by any means, mechanical or electronic, including photocopying or recording, or by any information storage and retrieval system, or transmitted by email without permission in writing from the author. Neither the author, editor or publisher assumes any responsibility for errors, omissions or contrary interpretations of the subject matter herein. Any perceived slight of any individual or organization is purely unintentional.

All Scripture quotations unless otherwise indicated, are taken from the Holy Bible, New International Version®, NIV®. Copyright © 1973, 1978, 1984, 2011 by Biblica, Inc.™ Used by permission of Zondervan. All rights reserved worldwide. www.zondervan.com The "NIV" and "New International Version" are trademarks registered in the United States Patent and Trademark Office by Biblica, Inc.™

Scripture taken from the New King James Version®. Copyright © 1982 by Thomas Nelson. Used by permission. All rights reserved.

Scripture quotations from the Authorized (King James) Version. Rights in the Authorized Version in the United Kingdom are vested in the Crown. Reproduced by permission of the Crown's patentee, Cambridge University Press.

Cover Design: Joanna Sanders LLC & Propel Marketing LLC
Editing: Joanna Sanders LLC
Layout & Formatting: Propel Marketing LLC
Author's Photo Credit: Diane Jones

ISBN 978-1-7353972-2-1
ISBN 978-1-7353972-3-8 (eBook)

Dedication

I dedicate this book to the following people, without whom this endeavor would not be possible:

To Diane, my beautiful wife of 36 years and counting,

To my wonderful children, Samantha, Laurel, and Hayley,

To my mom and dad,

To those who are with Jesus now but inspired this book: Pop, Nana, Uncle Fred, Roger and Vera, and Grandmom, and

To countless other seed planters along the way.

Contents

Introduction (Why I Wrote this Book) 11
Chapter 1: Discovering Treasure 21
Chapter 2: Letters from Dad 31
Chapter 3: Letters from Mom 51
Chapter 4: Letters from Diane's Folks 65
Chapter 5: Letters from Grandmom 83
Chapter 6: Letters from Pop.. 91
Chapter 7: Letter to Diane 129
Chapter 8: Letter to Samantha 135
Chapter 9: Letter to Laurel...139
Chapter 10: Letter to Hayley 143
Chapter 11: Treasures in Heaven 147
Chapter 12: Bob's Letter to You 161
About the Author 179

Introduction
(Why I Wrote this Book)

Since, then, you have been raised with Christ, set your hearts on things above, where Christ is, seated at the right hand of God. Set your minds on things above, not on earthly things. For you died, and your life is now hidden with Christ in God.

Colossians 3:1-3

FOR AN AVERAGE GUY, I'VE BEEN ACCUSED OF DOING SOME ODD THINGS. In my first book, I decided to take three decades of personal journaling and publish it for the world to see. Even my editor was surprised by this! In this, my second book, I am sharing some of the most meaningful letters I have received, and have written back some of the most intimate things I can share from my heart. Most people don't publish information of such a personal nature, and I can understand why.

I've come to understand that the nature of relationships needs to be so much deeper than "average." The letters I share in this book are from people whom I like to call "seed planters;" those who taught me about life and relationships long before I realized they were teaching me anything. Some of the letters, such as those to and from my children, are my very best attempt at leaving a legacy of what I've learned. And the letters to and from my wife could never adequately capture the more than three decades of our love. While I've done my best to declare her significance in my life, surely, I've fallen somewhat short. My greatest and most significant Teacher of all things "above average," however, has been my Lord and Savior Jesus Christ. And to give you the bottom-line up front (or, BLUF as we liked to call it in my previous business world), it is my hope that you hear and encounter His love woven here through letters that span generations of His goodness.

For many of us, our "average" or "normal" lives took on new meaning when a pandemic shut most of the world up in our homes in 2020. Much of the in-person communication that took place was moved to virtual platforms, texts, or emails. Churches and schools closed, and when we did see each other, social distancing and masks made the personal connection suddenly seem so impersonal. Like many of us, it wore on me after a while and a spirit of depression tried to settle in with me at home. It was during this exact season that God gave me a beautiful and unexpected breath of fresh air, in a stack of letters discovered from family and friends in what I now lovingly refer to as my "treasure chest." While some letters I vaguely remembered, all felt fresh to me. The letters were so personal, and the writers so invested in relationship and legacy. They breathed a wind of life into an average guy stuck in his house. And they made me appreciate the quickly fading art of communicating through handwritten letters.

When I was in college, many moons ago, I would regularly exchange letters with friends and family. It was common practice then. We had no other capability to communicate except by phone, and my dad was paying the phone bill during my college years with most of my calls being long-distance. If you're as old as I am you may remember how long-distance calling worked. You didn't dare call during the daytime unless it was a real emergency—it was extremely expensive! Depending on your phone company, you only had a certain window at night for reasonably-priced minutes. And those minutes could translate to significant dollars quickly if you talked for too long. Moreover, if Dad saw an anomaly on my phone bill, I heard about it immediately! So, it was easier to sit down and write a short letter. Oh, and Dad provided me with a roll of postage stamps before each semester, delivered appropriately with the strong (unspoken) hint to stay off the phone and write if I needed something.

I didn't hang on to my college letters so I don't remember most of the things that were written back then. The only thing I do recall is that I sent and received a good amount of mail. I do remember one cute card I received from a friend and it sticks out in my mind: On the front cover, the card said something like, "This morning I was thinking of you and I started to see spots in my eyes." Inside it read, "Then I realized that I had dozed off in my Raisin Bran" and it had a picture of a girl face-down in a bowl of cereal! I don't know why I recall things like this but it makes for a funny memory and another "Bob story" in the collection! It was always nice to get cards and letters from friends and family when I was away at college. Knowing that someone was thinking of me at home was encouraging and uplifting!

I still write the occasional letter to my parents or to others who need encouragement. I enjoy taking the time to let people know that they are loved and special. Truthfully, it's not always in my handwriting though. I'll also occasionally type letters on the computer and if you ever saw my penmanship, you'd understand that it's with good reason. My wife Diane occasionally reminds me of a grocery list I had once written. She perused the list and asked, "What are whipples?" I had trouble reading my own writing as well but eventually discerned that I was trying to write "waffles." Yes, my penmanship is *that* bad!

As I look back on these letters, I have been amazed to reflect on how much communication has changed even in my short life. I couldn't help but wonder, *have personal letters gone the way of the 45 record or cassette tape?* (If you're my age you'll remember those!) As a boy, I thought that the migration from black-and-white to color television was a big deal. And I couldn't have imagined that I could be hiking in the woods and use a device, not connected to any outlet or hard-wired phone line, to talk with someone miles away.

But with all of the gains due to technology, I believe that we may have lost some deeper things. Having been a leader in the business world I understand that our jobs can force us to continuously monitor our e-mails and phones. While some experts recommend checking e-mail only once or twice a day, the expectation in my career was to respond immediately, especially when a superior wrote to me. I often felt like Pavlov's Dog, reacting with attention at every "ding" and "beep" from my computer or phone. Associates would call me from the West Coast and say, "Didn't you get my e-mail, why didn't you respond?" I would look and discover that the e-mail was received about two minutes before the phone rang. Or, I could remember numerous times when colleagues and employees who sat in the next row would e-mail me rather than walk ten feet over to my office to talk in person. Unbelievable but true!

Of course, I understand that it is much easier and less time-consuming to write a few sentences or post a cute emoji on social media. And texts and e-mails are efficient methods of quick communication, especially in business. That's all fine and good, but, in my opinion, letters are more personal and imply that someone thought enough of me to take the time to write. There is just something about receiving that surprise letter in one's mailbox. And this coming from a guy who worked in the Information Technology (IT) field for over 20 years! I now wonder if we have allowed technology to replace personal interaction and deep relationships? Have we lost a little something with our short notes, our memes, and our quick methods of communication? Will the legacy of these be as impactful as we'd want them to be?

The book you are reading is a summary and a sampling of the treasures I discovered when I decided to search for old letters that my late grandfather, "Pop" had written to me years ago. The letters and corresponding stories are all true, real-life stuff. These family gems not only contain a rich history, but also precious memories and words of encouragement which I will cherish for the rest of my days. Several of my relatives have gone home to be with the Lord. These letters make it feel like a piece of them is still here with me. And God has used the messages in these letters to bloom what was planted earlier in my life. To be sure, I grew closer in my relationship with Jesus Christ when I wrote my first book, *Average Man, Almighty Companion*. And the same thing happened as I read these letters and wrote this book, which I believe was totally inspired by the Lord, Himself. It has helped me to live out Colossians 3:1 which is listed at the beginning of this introduction. As it was with *Average Man,* my desire again was to learn more about my Lord and to grow in my love and service for Him and for everyone I encounter in this journey called life.

Friend, if you can walk away with something from these letters, it would be what I have gained from my time with them: a reminder of the brevity and precious gift of this life, the importance of family, and the blessing of leaving a legacy for future generations. While these letters are such a treasure to me, I also want us to consider another question. What does it look like to store up treasures in heaven? What might that look like for you and me? Above all, I pray that the words will draw you closer to Jesus Christ and give you encouragement and hope.

Stories are important to me. I used stories throughout my career to articulate important points. They help us to recall information. Jesus often used stories and analogies in His teaching. I have included a number of stories in this book which came to mind as I read through the precious treasures I found. I want you to get a glimpse of the beautiful person behind the letters that God continues to use as a blessing in my life. I believe these stories will add a layer of new depth and meaning to the letters and the significance of how they were written.

Additionally, I have included pictorial images of actual letters from the treasure chest. These images will hopefully give you an even deeper, more intimate look into the lives of these precious relatives. Lastly, I have written a personal response to each family member who wrote to me many years ago. While a number of these dear loved ones are no longer with us, I have shared my heart of gratitude for their impact on my life.

Thank you for the honor of sharing these with you. I've prayed that the Lord would place this book in the hands of those who need this message. I also pray that there is something you can relate to in the many stories which will bless you as well.

Your friend,

Bob

So we fix our eyes not on what is seen, but on what is unseen, since what is seen is temporary, but what is unseen is eternal.
2 Corinthians 4:18

Chapter 1: Discovering Treasure

Do not store up for yourselves treasures on earth, where moths and vermin destroy, and where thieves break in and steal. But store up for yourselves treasures in heaven, where moths and vermin do not destroy, and where thieves do not break in and steal. For where your treasure is, there your heart will be also.

Matthew 6:19-21

THE MOMENTUM FOR THIS BOOK STARTED DURING A TIME WHEN I WAS FEELING SOMEWHAT STUCK. It was around the holidays, in the midst of more than six months of an almost-worldwide shutdown from the 2020 pandemic. Typically, the holidays reminded me of my late maternal grandfather, "Pop" who I consider to be a primary "seed planter" in my life. He and my grandmother "Nana" were such a big part of the holidays when I was growing up. I felt a sense of nostalgia and a bit of sadness as I fondly recalled those good times. He always spoke wisdom and encouragement into my life and his words have continued to impact the man I am today. As I considered Pop's godly example, his infectious smile, his sense of humor, and continual joyous spirit, I found myself longing to "hear" from him one more.

Then I remembered that he had written me a number of letters when I was younger. I had not thought about those letters in many years and I didn't know if I even had them anymore. I couldn't recall many details about what the letters contained except that he wrote to me from around 1983, when I graduated college and moved to Texas, to 1997 when he went home to be with Jesus. Those letters breathed fresh life into me after I moved away from home. I remember the feeling I had when I walked to the mailroom in my Texas apartment complex and discovered an envelope with Pop's name and return address. I can still imagine the thought, love, and intentionality I felt in his words.

While I don't believe in coincidences, I didn't know why these letters were coming to mind now but I longed to read them. In a real sense, I became obsessed with the desire to revisit Pop's letters. Perhaps they would bring me hope. Maybe God was bringing this to mind now to refocus my thoughts. I didn't understand why but perhaps somehow, I knew that they would breathe fresh life into me once more.

Yet, I had no idea where they were or even if Pop's letters were still in our possession. I knew if the letters still existed that they would be in our basement; a repository of Jones memorabilia which consists of elaborate labyrinths and rows of storage tubs. Consequently, I did what any wise husband would do: I asked my wife! I had not seen the letters in years but was relatively confident that we had them somewhere because Diane keeps everything! The question was, "Where?"

After several days of navigating a basement closet and digging through numerous plastic storage tubs, she produced a box which looked like a small treasure chest. Little did I know that what was inside would be worth more to me than gold.

Amazingly enough, I didn't rip into it. I found myself in reverence and awe of it, and I actually placed it on my desk and just stared at it for a while. It really was a sight. Leave it to my wife to have organized these precious letters in such an attractive way. It is an artistic box with an olive-colored cover, adorned with decorative writing and flowers, and a latch hook for closure. I decided to leave the treasure box unopened for another day. I wanted to give my full attention, without distraction, to reading the letters inside.

After several days, I moved the latch and lifted the convex lid. What I found inside was not a single treasure, but stacks of them. The box was not only filled with letters from Pop but also from several others as well. Unbeknownst to me, sometime in the past, Diane had saved and organized letters from a number of sources. She had also taken the time to carefully and lovingly wrap each set of letters with a pretty ribbon, tied into separate bows. The treasure chest was stuffed with letters!

The largest pile of treasure consisted of letters from Pop (with several notes from Nana and my great Uncle Fred). The stack measured almost four inches high! I also discovered packs of letters from my father, mother, paternal grandmother, Diane's parents, Diane's aunt and uncle, and even a former neighbor. I was so focused on locating Pop's letters I had forgotten that dad, mom, my paternal grandmother, and Diane's parents had also written to me. These letters were an added, unexpected blessing, further confirming that this box was tantamount to a treasure chest. What an exciting surprise! It was a little overwhelming as I viewed the stuffed box of letters. Where to begin?

I know it sounds funny, but being the type "A" personality I am, I felt that I needed a plan to go through this box. I decided to start with Dad's letters and meticulously work my way through the full box of letters, which, to my delight, took the better part of two weeks to get through them all. As I read through the precious memories and made notes, the words generated smiles, laughter, and a few tears. I was overwhelmed with gratitude that loved ones took the time to write during different seasons of my life. I was in my early twenties when relatives began to write letters, and much to my chagrin, I did not appreciate them like I did now. I was so busy trying to "find myself," while they were clearly planting seeds in my life and trying to guide me.

Even after reading the letters, one additional treasure remained in my box. I found the intangible proof that I had a Christian heritage from my late grandparents. You wouldn't know this from the way I was raised and the way I lived my life up through adulthood. And I certainly didn't realize it when I originally read the letters back then. But I now have the evidence. Jesus was working in my family long before I was born. He was orchestrating my path in the "Upper Story" even when life didn't make sense in my "Lower Story."

I was struck by the time and love which obviously went into the letters; imagining family members taking the time to think about me, sit down, and put pen to paper. And I thought about the now typical brevity of our regular communication, especially via text or "likes" over social media. Yet looking at these letters now brought a scripture to life for me in a new way. Proverbs 18:21 references that "the tongue has the power of life and death." As I realized the life these messages were still sparking in me, I couldn't help but consider if the writers could have imagined the impact of their letters. That's a powerful truth! Our words matter.

What's in Your Letter?

I am so grateful for family and friends with whom the Lord has blessed me and I often feel moved to write and express that as I can. I love to write letters of encouragement. I'll also write notes to say I'm thinking of and praying for friends and family who are struggling. Everyone needs encouragement and hope, and I think that is truer than ever during these times in which we live.

My wife and I have the incredible privilege to sponsor several children from less-fortunate countries. It is only by God's provision and blessing that we are in a position to help these dear children. He gets all of the glory for this. One of the greatest blessings to me is the letters we receive from these children.

Letters are the primary method of communication we have with these precious souls. I have no way of seeing their reactions to the short letters and pictures we send, and I may never get to meet any of them face-to-face. But I know how I feel when I receive a note from them, usually accompanied by hand-drawn pictures, colored in with crayons. The letters are personal and heartfelt. It is obvious that the child took the time and love to write out of sincere thanksgiving. I'm humbled and a bit ashamed at times at how much I take for granted. These children lack basic needs and appreciate the smallest gestures. One of our children wrote that the sponsorship kept his family from starving in 2020. That was enough to make me cry. I learn much from their faith and gratitude.

It is clear from the Bible that followers of Jesus Christ are called to sincerely care about people through our actions. I believe that, at least for me, letters are one way that I can love others in accordance with God's Word. The Bible exhorts and encourages us to invest in relationships by our words and actions. I'll share a few verses which inspire me in this way:

Gracious words are a honeycomb, sweet to the soul and healing to the bones.
Proverbs 16:24

And do not forget to do good and to share with others, for with such sacrifices God is pleased.
Hebrews 13:16

Carry each other's burdens, and in this way you will fulfill the law of Christ.
Galatians 6:2

Maybe it's been a long time since you have written or received an uplifting letter. Or perhaps you've never written or received one. Regardless of your situation, I encourage you to take the time and brighten someone's day with a personal note or letter. Phone calls, texts, and visits are also nice, and I would never get in the way of what God would specifically call you to do. But if you sense Him prompting you to reach out to someone, consider writing a letter.

I am so thankful for these letters that I now possess as a permanent treasure. It's never too late to start. The love and memories will create treasures of a lifetime for you and for generations to come.

I remember the days of long ago; I meditate on all your works and consider what your hands have done.
Psalm 143:5

Chapter 2: Letters from Dad

Remember the days of old; consider the generations long past. Ask your father and he will tell you, your elders, and they will explain to you.

Deuteronomy 32:7

After Dad had his first stroke in 2011, I realized that I knew very little about him. Dad did not typically volunteer information about his past and was generally a private person. It was startling, as an adult, to realize that I didn't know much at all about his childhood, his upbringing, his military service, nor how he and Mom even met. I had a deep desire to know him more and was so thankful that he was open enough to explain his life story to me as I sat down and interviewed him one day.

Dad grew up in humble, very tough economic circumstances. He lived in five different homes in southern New Jersey, literally across the river from Philadelphia. He and his family faced hardships that are foreign to me and many today who are blessed to live in the United States. In spite of the trials and hard times, Dad never felt sorry for himself; he was determined to help his family, support himself, and live a better life. To that end, as a kid, he did all types of odd jobs to earn money. He actually earned enough money to buy his own car and pay for the insurance when he was in high school. This was not a common occurrence in those times.

His work ethic and sense of personal responsibility allowed him to eventually move from a life of poverty into a successful middle-class career. His parents could not afford college for him, so his dream of becoming a dentist never came to fruition. He would have made a good one, in my opinion. Dad had the intelligence, but unfortunately not the resources. He was a whiz at math and technically smart as well. I don't think that Dad has any regrets though. He played the cards he was dealt and worked hard to succeed, in spite of the obstacles.

For as long as I can remember, Dad worked two jobs from Monday through Friday. Every work day, he would leave early in the morning and not return home until after 10 p.m. He also worked a shift on his second job from noon until 10 p.m. on Saturdays. Sunday was literally the only day he was home for the entire day, and he expected order in the house. I don't know how he had the energy and initiative to keep that kind of schedule, but he did it. Prior to that, he also served our country honorably in the military and excelled there.

When Dad retired in his fifties, he wanted to move to a rural area where he could have several acres of land and some farm animals. Dad had spent time on his aunt's farm growing up and dreamed of this kind of life as a retirement goal. This was quite the change from our life next to the city of Philadelphia. He simply wanted to get away from city life and enjoy retirement in the country. After buying and selling several properties, he and Mom settled on a property in southern Virginia where they remain today.

On his property in Virginia, he plowed and fenced in acres of pasture to care for horses, donkeys, chickens, guinea hens, and even a llama. Yes, a real llama. This was obviously a new education for me as well. I'm showing my ignorance but I didn't know what a "guinea hen" was until the first time I visited their farm! These ground-based fowl perpetually ran around the property and I wondered aloud about their purpose in life. Mom told me that they ate ticks and were good for the farm. I would still find ticks on myself and Diane though, so I was incredulous at this claim; either the farm had more ticks than the hens could ingest or they weren't really the tick-hunters Mom claimed they were!

As was in his career, even in "retirement," Dad's work ethic remained unstoppable. In addition to caring for the farm, Dad also worked full-time as a high school driving instructor about thirty miles from the farm. He got to know many high school students in the area and made a positive difference in their lives. Even today, Dad will encounter former students in the community, and they express their gratitude to him. I'm exhausted thinking about the magnitude of work he accomplished on his property and in his community, *after* he "retired!"

With Dad's upbringing, it would have been understandable if he were frugal with his money, but he always demonstrated generosity when it came to his family and helping others. He taught me to tip well for good service and to "be a sport" whenever I took a girl on a date. If I asked him for $5 to cover gas for my car, Dad would give me $10. He also helped friends and acquaintances who struggled financially. His example of generosity is a character trait I try to model today. And now I recognize it as a Biblical principle as well.

Clearly, Dad always set a high standard. He excelled at whatever he did, but never desired praise or recognition. He just quietly, consistently did his best at everything he attempted. He managed his responsibilities and commitments. He could fix anything around the house. I don't know if I fully appreciated it when I was younger but we never lacked any material needs as a family. At the time when I was a boy, I took this for granted. I didn't realize until much later that Dad's experience growing up was one of want and poverty. He worked tirelessly to give his family the things he didn't have as a child. He taught me personal responsibility and the rewards of hard work.

His expectations of me, as the firstborn child, were lofty though. I feared my father; he was stoic and strict, and had a short fuse which I had a tendency to light. While I tried my best to live up to being the perfect son, it was a lot to shoulder and I felt like I failed continually! He expected me to "act like a man," before I really knew what that meant. I could put on a good front, but my thoughts, attitude, and tongue often left much to be desired. I seldom felt like I was "good enough" and that I had to prove myself over and over. It was not a healthy way to live. To be honest, before I was rescued by Jesus Christ, it didn't take much to push my buttons as well. In my teen years, Dad did not react well when anything was out of order.

I distinctly remember one summer when I was home on college break. I worked second shift at a factory which corrugated paper into cardboard and cardboard into boxes. Hours were tracked by timeclock and there was zero tolerance for tardiness or leaving early. I was on my way to work one summer afternoon when a woman ran into the back of my car; my old AMC Hornet. My car had 3-speed on the column so I learned to drive a stick shift out of necessity. I bought the car because it was cheap and got me where I needed to go. (Well, most, but not all times! That's a story in itself.)

On this particular day I was sitting at a stop sign, waiting for traffic to clear before pulling onto a main thoroughfare, when the accident happened. The woman was distracted and hit me without even braking. I never saw it coming. Fortunately, no one was hurt but my car had significant damage.

The police arrived and questioned each of us. The woman admitted that the accident was her fault. I tried to move things along because I didn't want to be late for work. Once the officer had all of our information and issued the woman a summons, I headed to work and barely made it on time. The metal from the rear of my car was pushed in to the point where it touched the back wheels whenever I hit a bump in the road. The car needed obvious repair but it was "drive-able." Even though the accident was not my fault, I dreaded making the call to inform my dad. Again, he didn't like it when the "apple cart" was upset and I feared his reaction.

During my dinner break at work, I was in the company cafeteria and called my dad on a pay phone (yes, I'm showing my age) to tell him what had happened. He was working his second job and became obviously upset with the news of my accident. After several minutes, I looked out of the cafeteria window and noticed that Dad had pulled up into the parking lot. He walked around my car to assess the damage. I could tell from his body language that he was not happy and I wasn't sure what I would face when I got home.

My natural reaction was to blame myself, even though there was nothing I could have done to avoid the accident (except perhaps stay home). A coworker noticed that I was visibly upset, at both the trauma from the accident itself and my dad's reaction. But the right words, spoken at the right time, are healing. My friend said something like: "Bob, when you look back in a month this isn't going to mean anything." And he was correct! I have never forgotten those words. Although the damage was over $1000 (a lot of money then) and slightly less than I paid for the car, the vehicle was fixed in less than a week. Moreover, the woman's insurance paid for the damage to my car. Dad got over being upset quickly and really helped coordinate the repairs with the body shop. In the end, all was well, just as my friend predicted it would be. Please understand, I don't tell this story to belittle my dad in any way but to demonstrate how the Lord has transformed his heart (and mine).

Knowing more about Dad's past gave me perspective about how I was raised. Dad was hard to get to know and I feared him much of the time. He wasn't "available" often due to his work responsibilities. I might not have observed a sensitive, compassionate side to Dad as I was growing up, but I also had (and still have) tremendous respect for him. Amazingly, I watched God soften his heart when I moved from home to my first career in Texas. I saw his heart soften even more when his grandchildren came into the picture. Looking back, I am amazed at the relationship we have now compared to what it was like growing up. I do not know how much of who we become is due to "nature" or "nurture" but I am sure of this: the person Dad was, is not who he is now. And the person I was growing up is not the person I am now and it's solely because of the love, grace, mercy, and patience of my Lord and Savior, Jesus Christ. We both carry remnants of our old selves but we are totally different people today, thanks be to God! One of my favorite verses in the Bible describes this transformation that only God can render: "Therefore, if anyone is in Christ, he is a new creation; old things have passed away; behold, all things have become new" (2 Corinthians 5:17, NKJV).

At the end of my interview of him, Dad discussed his first stroke that he had in 2011. He said, "I thank God each morning that I'm able to wake." Dad had a severe second stroke in 2016. I am so thankful that I got to know him more before that occurred. That stroke has taken its toll but Dad has not given up. He is a fighter. Dad is still one of the smartest and toughest people I know. He is also the hardest working person I've ever known. I have the utmost love and respect for my dad. He is my hero.

Today, Dad and Mom live a little over five hours from us so we don't have the opportunity to visit as much as I would like. My parents can no longer visit us due to health issues so our face-to-face contact is limited. My dad is not a man of many words on the phone so I write frequently out of gratitude and to offer encouragement to both parents. My plan for 2020 was to visit once a month but the circumstances of the year limited our trips. Whenever we visit, I love the conversations and fellowship with my parents. But in between visits, the phone calls and texts are just not the same. I find that personal letters allow me to express my love and feelings in detail. And I know that the letters lift Mom and Dad's spirits tremendously.

Dad has forgotten more than I will ever know about a lot of things and his support and example allowed me to have a better life. Knowing Dad's past taught me two valuable lessons:

First, we should never judge someone at face value; you and I don't always know what a person has experienced and do not walk in their shoes. We all react differently to trials. Once I understood Dad's upbringing and childhood, it provided perspective and empathy.

Second, and most significantly, God can radically change anyone's life, no matter their past. I want to thank Him for the transformation in Dad's life as indicated in the letters he wrote to me, starting when I was in Texas. I know Dad much better now, am so grateful that he is still alive, and have the treasure of his letters to bless me for the rest of my life. These treasures will also be passed on to my children and future generations.

As I dove into the treasure chest and started to read Dad's letters, I recalled that he would periodically send me little notes when I was in college. Most days when I checked my mailbox in the College Center, it was empty. The small student mailboxes couldn't hold much more than one or two standard envelopes. If a student received anything larger, a small note was placed in the mailbox. The note stated something like, "See clerk for package." The mail office had limited hours so sometimes I had to wait a day if there was a package for me to pick up. If I arrived too late on a Friday, I would have to wait until Monday.

Each tiny mailbox had a clear window so one could tell just by looking from the outside whether or not mail was present. There was no need to open the combination lock if I didn't see a shadow in the box. Being totally honest, each time I checked for mail I always hoped that there was something in the box from home. My spirits were always lifted when I received mail. I had this same type of anticipation when I first saw the treasure box!

Dad's notes were succinct but always welcomed, encouraging, and comforting. I went to college outside of New York City, about two hours from our home near Philadelphia. Although I travelled home most weekends to play in a band, I still spent the majority of my time on campus, with very little money. Any money I made from the band or summer jobs went for tuition. I didn't qualify for a credit card back then and my only safety net was a check Dad gave me "for emergencies only." I ended up using that check during my junior year, the day I started an internship at a large multinational corporation which was about 30 miles from campus. I pulled the old AMC Hornet into the parking lot of the office building and the clutch went out. That kind of spoiled my first day on the job! I had to use Dad's check to pay for the tow and the new clutch.

Dad would often tuck a $5 bill in with his notes. The note would read something like, "Rob, hope your week is going well. Have a pizza on me." Now, five dollars may not seem like a lot of money today, but for a broke college kid back then, it could purchase multiple cups of coffee, snacks, and enough gas to get home! I felt rich whenever I received a note from Dad! Unfortunately, I don't have any of those notes from my college days but I never forgot about Dad's thoughtfulness and generosity.

As I read his letters again, I was reminded that Dad was proud of me. I didn't always hear or feel this growing up but it was heartwarming to see the proof in writing now. We are never too old for encouragement and uplifting words. My brother and sister can speak for themselves but I know that Dad is proud of them as well; each of them has unique gifts, strong work ethics, and special relationships of their own with my parents.

The earliest letters I found are the ones Dad wrote to me when I first moved to Texas. Dad drove me from New Jersey to Texas after I graduated college and began my first career. Mom flew to Texas a few days later and joined us. I was so grateful that my parents helped to get me set up in an apartment, with provisions, as I started my first real career. On the day they said "goodbye" to drive home to New Jersey, we all got pretty emotional. Seeing my dad shed tears was hard to process because I had never seen that emotion from him prior to that. That event turned out to be one of many heart-softening, turning points in my journey towards the ultimate rescue by Jesus Christ.

Dad's first letters, when I was living in Texas, confirmed how much my parents missed me and wanted the best for my life. Those letters were comforting as I read them. I didn't realize until I read the letters that Mom checked the mail at home every day and was disappointed when I didn't write. During that time, I had just met Diane and we were dating so I'm sure that I was self-absorbed. The love in those letters hit me as I read them again, knowing that my parents (and siblings) missed and thought about me.

Diane and I met in Texas in July of 1983, on the first day of class for an internship in a large organization. I proposed to her in October of that same year. Interestingly, we did not immediately announce our engagement to any family members except for my dad. The plan was to fly home for Christmas, meet each other's parents, and announce the engagement then. Diane's hometown was in northern Pennsylvania and mine in southern New Jersey. I don't remember why I singled out my dad to share our engagement news, but I did. As I think about it now, it shows how close my relationship with Dad had grown. Diane and I did not plan to fly from Texas to our respective homes for

Thanksgiving. We both had little money and were just getting started in our careers.

Dad, always the generous one, wanted to surprise my mother at Thanksgiving. He loved orchestrating surprises but he, (like me), just didn't like being on the receiving end of them! So, he proposed the idea of flying Diane and me to my New Jersey home. He insisted on purchasing the airline tickets with the condition that we didn't tell anyone. Thinking about it now, Dad must have had a great deal of trust in me, to accept Diane "sight unseen." I have two letters in the treasure box from Dad providing instructions for our "secret visit." Dad also bribed his mom, Grandmom Jones (more about her a little later), to cook an extra turkey because the entire family, including grandparents, were expected to be present at the Thanksgiving meal. And somehow, we managed to keep the trip a secret!

The trip home for Thanksgiving that year was unforgettable. The day prior to Thanksgiving, Diane and I drove from east Texas to Dallas for a flight to Philadelphia. Dad met us at the airport in Philly. It was wonderful to see him after being away for four months, and he made Diane feel welcome immediately. Mom was surprised when I walked in the door late on the Wednesday evening before Thanksgiving. She was even more surprised that a young lady followed me into the house. Then I sprung the news that Diane and I were engaged! I spent time with my siblings and grandparents while we were home. The entire experience was a great blessing!

Dad wrote a letter right after we left New Jersey to return to Texas. I received it in early December. Dad was so touched by the visit and wrote, "...let each experience be a lesson that someday you may get the opportunity to 'teach' someone else. It's a great feeling..." I was so blessed to read this treasure, and doubly-blessed that I can go back to these words any time I need encouragement. I've taken those words to heart, not only to teach my children, but also to encourage those I encounter in my journey.

Dad wrote additional letters to me while I was in Texas and continued the practice once Diane and I had children. He wrote several letters to Diane and the girls when I was away on business travel. It's funny, Dad's penmanship has always been impeccable. He prints each word and the letters are clear, neat, and perfect. I did not inherit that gift! I often joke that I could have been a doctor based on my handwriting (have you ever seen the way some prescriptions are written?). Only a few things held me back from that dream, e.g., grades, intelligence, high school math, etc. Seriously though, even after two strokes which affected my dad mentally and physically, his penmanship is still flawless!

Something else I didn't know about Dad and learned in our interview: He is a gifted poet. He had more than fifty poems copyrighted and was even a finalist in a national poetry contest. Dad's poems blessed a number of his acquaintances through the years. At Christmas time in 1994, Dad penned a poem for all of his grandkids. It was a blessing to read the poems. Dad put so much love and thought into them.

In 1995, Dad mailed us a copy of a letter that he had sent to Diane's parents, one of the few he wrote in cursive. When I read this letter, it brought me to tears. Dad said how wonderful Diane and the kids were and how proud he was of me. Reading the words now makes me feel like I did something right as a child, despite my flaws and the labels I placed on myself. I can only thank God for all He has done for us all.

It is difficult for me to articulate how much of a blessing these letters were to me as I read them again. After more than thirty years of following Jesus Christ, I have a clear glimpse of Dad's heart. I can't say that I fully appreciated the letters at the time they were written, but I am so grateful for the treasure now.

One final note to express how much I appreciated my father's words. Many times, in my adult years, I would call Dad if I had a problem which seemed insurmountable. It may have been an issue at work, a financial concern, worries about the kids, you name it. Just hearing Dad say, "You'll be fine Rob, it will all work out," was enough to give me peace about my situation, regardless of the issue. I got the same feeling as I read these treasures, like it was the first time.

I thank God for this treasure and the positive power of words. His Word, the Holy Bible, confirms that the right words, spoken at the right time, in a loving way, will always be a blessing.

A word fitly spoken is like apples of gold in settings of silver.
Proverbs 25:11 (NKJV)

My Letter to Dad

Dear Dad,

I've heard it said that we get to choose our friends but we don't choose our families. When I look back at the big picture, I'm grateful that God chose to give you to me as my earthly father. Growing up had its ups and downs and many times I did not make it easy. But God and time have healed the things I've chosen to forget. God had something bigger planned. He was working in the Upper Story, as He always has, to water the seeds that were planted. Thank you for teaching me the Biblical principles you may not have even realized you taught: hard work, personal responsibility, and respect for others. Above all, thank you for modelling and teaching me how to be generous to others.

Your letters, notes, and succinct advice continue to guide me and I'm a better man for those things. I thank God that I am still blessed to have you at this stage of my life. I love you and pray for you continually. You are my hero.

Love,

Rob

One of Dad's letters prior to our surprise visit Thanksgiving of 1983. I had forgotten that my dad often referred to me as "Rober" (pronounced "Row-Bear").

Dear Rober and Diane: November 16, 1983

    Just a short note to say hi. This will be my last correspondence prior to your arrival next Wednesday. Mom is still convinced that she will not be seeing you both until Christmas.

    Grandmom Jones is cooking an extra turkey for the large number of people we'll be having over for dinner. Mom wants me to send you a floral arrangement for your Thanksgiving Dinner table so I'll have to fake it somehow.

    I am going to come to my office this Sunday, at 6:30 PM. Give me a call at 609-███-████ so we can discuss final arrangements for the trip home.

    The picture looked great, we are all looking forward to meeting Diane at Christmas (OOPS) I mean Thanksgiving.

    Take care and make a note of your call to me. 6:30 PM sharp.

Take care

Love

Dad

Chapter 3: Letters from Mom

Our mouths were filled with laughter, our tongues with songs of joy. Then it was said among the nations, "The LORD has done great things for them."

Psalm 126:2

UNTIL I OPENED THIS TREASURE CHEST, I didn't realize that Mom had written so many letters to me. Dad's letters were on the shorter side. Mom tended to write longer letters. Her letters typically consisted of several pages, sometimes as many as seven! Her stack in the treasure chest was the second largest, about half the size of Pop's. She started writing to me after I moved to Texas. Her letters made me smile as I read through them. Mom's penmanship is slightly better than mine (read "barely legible"). I'm exaggerating a bit, but Mom wrote strictly in cursive and I had to concentrate to make sense of it all. This makes me empathize with people who have tried to decipher my own handwriting!

My dear mother was born in Philadelphia and raised in southern New Jersey. She worked in Philadelphia with one of my aunts who ultimately introduced Dad to Mom after he returned from military service. To return the favor, Dad introduced my late uncle (who was in the service with dad) to that same aunt!

My mother did some freelance work when the kids were small but was primarily a stay-at-home mom until I was a teenager. She then had a very successful career in sales. It sounds like a cliché but she could sell anything to anyone, and she always did so with honesty and integrity. She cultivated many friendships with clients and still keeps in contact with several of them.

Mom wrote me frequently when I moved to Texas. She kept me abreast of things at home and for some reason missed me being nearby. (I say this tongue-in-cheek based on my antics as a child!) The college I attended was only two hours away and I drove home most weekends to play in a band. Texas was different, though. I was no longer in New Jersey but approximately 1300 miles away, in another time zone. I would never return to their home to live after that. It was a turning point in my life and

Mom's letters always helped to alleviate homesickness, especially during the first few months after I moved.

Unlike Dad, Mom is more of an extrovert and has never been one to mind her own business. I say this lovingly, in a good way. Frankly, though, her outgoing personality bothered me a little when I was younger. After all, I'm an introvert and in my natural state, just want to be left alone. I could be home on a college break and Mom would see someone in the store and say, "Rob, there's so-and-so, you remember her don't you, go say hi." I'd respond, "I don't remember her, let's keep walking." She'd respond, "Yes you do, she lived on such and such a street," and on and on the dialogue would go.

Now, the last thing I wanted to do was get into an awkward conversation with someone who was likely no more than an acquaintance. And I was being honest when I told my mom that I really didn't remember the person she was pointing out. Have you ever had the pleasure of thinking you recognized someone and called their name, only to have them turn around and be someone else? I've done that more than a few times and it's always embarrassing! For that reason, unless I am 100% sure that I know the person, I'll wait until they recognize me first. I love people and cherish relationships. But I'm awkward on my own until I really know someone. I rely heavily on God's help in my interactions with people.

Mom had a lot of sayings for me when I was younger as well. One of my favorites, when I misbehaved as a child, was this one: "Rob, you need to turn over a new leaf," which says something about my "old leaf" (bad behavior). Mom had another one that comes to mind: "You're making a mountain out of a molehill!" Honestly, I don't know if I've ever seen a molehill so it took me awhile to understand the metaphor. A few years ago, we had an infestation of "voles" (not moles) in our front yard, but they didn't make any "vole hills," just a labyrinth of tunnels. But I came to understand the gist of Mom's saying; we can imagine that every little issue is comparable to a mountain we must climb, meaning it's not as bad as we make it out to be. The lesson stuck with me. Perspective is important.

I had been in Texas for a little over a week when Mom wrote a very nice letter to me. I was still adjusting to a new town and career, and a new girlfriend. With all of these life changes happening simultaneously, letters from home were certainly a welcome sight. I think that I had been dating Diane for about a week and I mentioned to my parents that I had met someone. In her August 1983 letter, Mom wrote that I "seemed pretty serious about her." Mom didn't stop there though; she also enclosed a note for Diane. While I appreciate the fact that Mom is very comfortable in her own skin (something I struggle with personally), this was too soon in my mind! Mom had never even met Diane in person!

Part of me wanted to just keep the letter to myself but Diane was (and is) so sweet and understanding that I knew she would take it the right way. As I think about it now, Mom's reaction also reflected trust in my choices. She wanted Diane to feel welcome and to also share some nice things about me in the letter. I don't care who you are, we all could use an encouraging word from time-to-time. In a letter about a month later, Mom wrote, "I hope she likes us..." I knew that this would not be an issue; Diane can get along with anyone and my mom has a loving, friendly personality.

While I was living in Texas, Mom and Dad had bought and sold several properties in rural Virginia. A letter from October 8, 1993 really made me laugh, and I didn't remember this at all as I re-read through the treasures. My parents drove from New Jersey to Virginia to visit the property they planned to buy. On their way, near Washington, DC, they encountered a detour from the interstate due to an accident. They did not have the benefit of GPS then! They ended up on a long dirt road which paralleled the Potomac River. After they stopped and asked one man for directions, Dad was frustrated and wanted to turn around and head home. The man had no idea how to direct my parents to their destination. Mom convinced Dad to go a little further on the dirt road.

Thankfully, Dad noticed some people congregated in a park and stopped to ask for help. One of the men was gracious enough to share a map with Dad. The helpful man also told my dad that he was not far from a ferry which could shuttle them and their small Datsun 200SX across the Potomac into Virginia. Dad took the man's suggestion and soon arrived at the loading zone.

The ferry (i.e., a glorified, motorized raft from what I can surmise) was on the other side of the river but soon returned to the dock. The man running the boat directed two cars on and motioned for Dad to pull in behind one of the autos. Evidently there was room on the ferry for one more vehicle after Dad parked his car, so a lady drove a pick-up truck onto the boat. The truck was towing a trailer which contained a large horse. As the woman proceeded onto the ferry deck, her truck scraped the side of my parents' vehicle and the horse trailer got hooked on their bumper. I can just picture Dad; I'm sure that he was "having kittens!"

In the letter, my mom writes: "The guy was yelling for her to stop but this lady was in 'Spaceville'. All the way across the river we stayed hooked on the horse trailer. When they unloaded the cars off on the Virginia side of the river, the guy tried directing Dad off, but every time we tried, the horse came with us. Finally, another man who was mowing the grass came over and suggested lifting dad's car off the trailer. Several guys physically lifted the car and moved it enough that we could drive off. They have to replace the bumper and fix the side of the car. The lady had no insurance card so they exchanged numbers. Surprisingly Dad was mad at first but then we laughed about it." I didn't remember the aforementioned story at all but I called Mom after I read it and we had a good laugh.

This story reminded me of a fishing trip I took with Dad and one of his work friends when I was younger. Dad's friend supplied the boat which he had towed to the New Jersey bay using his pickup truck and a trailer. When we were done fishing, Dad tried to help his friend get the boat from the water onto the trailer, which was backed up to the bay. As soon as Dad stepped onto the wet boat ramp, he slipped and slid right into the bay, barely missing the trailer and avoiding possible injury. I was shocked at first but held back laughter. He tried a second time and fell again, and this time I laughed audibly which made Dad a little mad. After he fell in the third time, he couldn't help but laugh as well. Eventually the friend was able to maneuver the boat onto the trailer and thankfully only Dad's ego was bruised.

My dear mother has done some unintentional funny things in her life. I could probably write an entire book on those stories! Once, when she and Dad were going on vacation, they dropped their dog off at a boarding establishment. The owner placed the dog in a shelter which had a doggy door leading to an outside, confined area. Mom was apprehensive about leaving the dog, so the owner tried to make Mom feel at ease; he invited her into the building to say one last "goodbye" to the dog before leaving. Mom misunderstood his directions and proceeded to enter the confined area, crouch down and crawl through the doggy door to say her farewell to the pooch!

To appreciate the humor my mom brings, I'll share one last "Mom" story. Mom had won tickets from a Philadelphia radio station to see a very famous rock-and-roll icon in concert. I think I was in college then, so Mom took my younger sister, who was sixteen at the time, to the venue. The show ran late and it was almost 11 p.m. when the artist performed the final song. Due to the late hour and work the next day, Mom decided that she and my sister would leave during the last song to get ahead of the crowd. As the song began, Mom made her way to the end of the row and the last thing she remembers is somehow stumbling and landing in the balcony aisle. She had tripped on her coat, broken a heel, and rolled down several rows before coming to a stop.

The commotion caught the singer's attention, which was evident when he paused from singing and stopped the whole concert. He looked at the upper deck of the theater and announced, "Is everyone okay up there?" Mom was dazed from the fall and hobbled on a missing heel but gave the "thumbs up" and the concert continued. In Mom's condition she was unable to drive, so my unlicensed sister took the wheel and thankfully got them both back home. As Mom says, "No permanent damage except my shoes!"

There are so many stories like that and they all have made me smile at just the right moments. That's my dear mother and I would not change her for the world!

Mom continued to write letters after she and Dad moved to the farm in Virginia permanently. In 1995, Mom wrote that she was enjoying life on the farm and the kids and grandkids visiting. I was blessed to read this at the end of Mom's letter: "Pray for one another. Prayer changes things." I was relatively new in my Christian walk so I didn't fully appreciate Mom's words back then. Those words mean so much now. I am so grateful for the work the Lord has done in my parents' lives. The unexpected treasure of her letters will live on well beyond this life.

A cheerful heart is good medicine, but a crushed spirit dries up the bones.
Proverbs 17:22

My Letter to Mom

Dear Mom,

Thank you for your unconditional love and support since the day I was born. I know that I wasn't the best son in the world, especially in my younger years. But you planted many good seeds and I'd like to think that your love, patience, grace, and continual encouragement helped those seeds to bloom in my life.

Your sayings and sense of humor have always blessed me. You've also had your share of health issues and surgeries but you keep fighting and making the best of your circumstances. Thank you for the love you have for Diane and your grandchildren. Thank you most of all for a Godly heritage, one that wasn't obvious nor practiced in our family, but something God used to build a foundation of faith in my life.

May God continue to bless you and Dad.

With all of my love, your son,

Rob

This is one of several letters Mom wrote to Diane when we first started dating in Texas. Mom would not meet Diane until our surprise visit for Thanksgiving in 1983.

> Dear Diane,
>
> It was a pleasure meeting you even though it was "via" the telephone. Hopefully, I didn't come across as overbearing. My children have been a great source of joy to me & I love them all dearly.
>
> Anyway, I just wanted to say thanks for being such a good friend to Rob. He really is a special person. (There I go again!)

If he hasn't as yet, get him to sing & play the guitar for you. I miss hearing his voice.

It's kind of early to ask you, but you are most welcome to join us on Christmas Day for dinner or any time that you can manage during the holidays.

The best of luck to you in your career.

Regards,
Shirley Jones

Chapter 4: Letters from Diane's Folks

Above all, love each other deeply, because love covers over a multitude of sins.

1 Peter 4:8

THE LETTERS FROM MY IN-LAWS WERE AN UNEXPECTED SURPRISE THAT I DID NOT REMEMBER. Perhaps the reason is that most of them were written to Diane. I knew that she would be okay with me reading these treasures but I asked for her approval anyway. Advice to husbands: Always be open and honest with your wife! It's Biblical and the right thing to do. I was seeing some of these letters for the first time. Diane is an only child and was very close with her dear parents. For this reason, these letters are extremely intimate and heartfelt.

I did not meet Diane's parents until Christmas 1983. She had called her parents during the Thanksgiving holiday (during the visit to my parents' New Jersey home) that year to announce our engagement, but we would not meet face-to-face until Christmas time. Their acceptance of me "sight-unseen" is a testament to the trust they had in Diane's choices.

In December of that year, Diane and I had an extended break from our internship in Texas so we travelled from Dallas-Fort Worth Airport to Philadelphia. Both Diane's and my parents also met for the first time at the Philly airport. After a short time of greetings, Diane and I went our separate ways, she to northern Pennsylvania and I to southern New Jersey.

During the break I drove from my parents' home to Diane's house and got lost when I was a few miles from my destination. Sometimes she'll joke with me, "When you saw where I grew up, I'm surprised you didn't keep driving!" Truthfully, I loved her hometown from the time I first visited. And I loved her parents from the moment we met. They made me feel at home; like a son, from day one.

Both Diane's dad Roger and mother Vera wrote a number of letters to Diane when she lived in Texas. After we were married her parents wrote to me and our children as well. Vera loved to read newspaper and magazine articles. In her letters to Diane, she often included news clippings as well as store coupons. She also wrote about the neighborhood "gossip" which Diane enjoyed. It wasn't gossip in a negative sense, just the update on everyone in their small town. Having grown up literally across the river from Philadelphia, I loved visiting Diane's hometown where I experienced the feeling of small-town life.

Diane's dad Roger was very generous to us in spite of limited financial resources. When we purchased our first home, he insisted on helping us with the down payment. I'll never forget what he said to me: "Bob, you need the money now, not when I'm dead."

Roger also helped us with the down payment for our second home. We had the funds and didn't ask for the help, but he surmised that the extra money would make our mortgage payment lower. He was right, of course. In my pride I insisted that it be treated as a loan which I would pay back. A few years later, Roger wrote me a note, listing all of the work he had done for us and the financial assistance he and Vera had provided to us. At the bottom of the letter, he had written in big letters, "Paid in Full." I had done nothing to earn this gift nor to pay any of it back myself. This reminded me of another debt, a much bigger one, which was paid by Jesus Christ for me and you (John 19:30).

The magnitude of Roger's sacrificial generosity really hit home for me when I read his letter to Diane from February 23, 1984. Diane and I were still living in Texas and planned to get married in October of that year. Roger was a carpenter by trade and work was often seasonal in that field. Typically, he had carpentry jobs for part of the year but was laid off for months at a time, especially in the winter. This translated to limited income, but, knowing his laid-back personality, I can't imagine that he was stressed out about this situation. He did the best he could to find freelance work when big jobs were not available and he made the most of any down time. He helped his neighbors with little jobs and loved spending time with Diane. He and Vera did a wonderful job raising her and I am humbled and privileged to be her husband.

Roger wrote in his letter that he had sent our engagement picture to his local paper. He also said that he had to work three more jobs to pay for our wedding but that "we meant a lot to him." This was humbling as I read it and brought tears to my eyes. He had helped us so much over the years but I had no idea until now of the extent to which he sacrificed so much from the beginning of our marriage. Roger knew how much I appreciated his love and support for us over the years, but this letter made my respect and gratitude grow even deeper, if that's possible.

One of the many things I loved about Roger was his sense of adventure. When Diane was accepted into the same intern program as I was (recall that we did not meet until our first day of class), Roger accompanied Diane to Texas and made the most of the trip. He shared driving responsibilities with Diane on the long journey from northern Pennsylvania. Roger ensured that he and Diane experienced every significant tourist attraction along the way, including Mud Island in Memphis, Tennessee.

They drove Diane's large 8-cylinder Chevy Impala. This tank, which I believe was from the late 60s/early 1970s, guzzled gas like crazy and had 4-60 air conditioning—meaning you had to roll down all four windows and drive 60 miles-per-hour just to try to stay cool! I fondly referred to that behemoth as "Big Blue." By the time Big Blue crossed the border from Tennessee into Arkansas, it was so hot in the car that Diane resorted to pouring cups of cold water over her head to attempt to cool off.

On a side note, we kept "Big Blue" for the first couple years of our marriage and I continually made jokes about its size and poor gas mileage. That is, until one day when the battery died in my car and we had no other transportation to our workplace but Big Blue. I ate humble pie that day and Diane reminded me of this whenever I complained about her car!

Roger stayed with Diane for a few days in east Texas, said his goodbye, and took a bus to Dallas. He toured the city and made sure that he visited Texas Stadium, a real highlight of the trip for him. Subsequently, he caught a train back to Pennsylvania. He made the most of every experience. I always loved Roger's sense of adventure and his appreciation of the simple things.

Right before Diane and I left Texas to move to central New Jersey for our careers in the spring of 1984, Roger ventured out on a road trip with Diane's uncle Gerry. The two started out early one fine morning from their homes in northern Pennsylvania to the town where Diane and I would be working in New Jersey. Roger wanted to check out the office building and the layout of the area. I don't remember this letter but do remember the picture of the office building Roger sent to Diane. The letter starts out this way: "Hi Diane, I guess this will be my last letter to you while in Texas (Goodbye Texas, thank God)." Roger, always a stickler for details, enclosed a hand-drawn picture of the building where we would be working, complete with intricate depictions of the entrance, parking lots, and entry/exit roads.

He and Diane's uncle left Pennsylvania at 8 a.m. that morning and didn't get home until 12:30 a.m. the next day. They had driven a total of 503 miles and Roger provided details of every road they travelled. After visiting the office building, he stopped and talked to people about potential places where Diane and I could live when we moved to New Jersey. They stopped at a fast-food restaurant for lunch before heading to Atlantic City, New Jersey. Roger's brother turned down dinner at another fast-food joint in favor of a lounge near Atlantic City.

Gerry, Roger's brother, learned that free food was being served at the lounge's "Happy Hour" and he remarked several times about how impressed he was with the bounty. After walking the boardwalk and through a few of the hotel casinos, they stopped for snacks and headed home. The last thing Roger mentioned was the toll roads, but "it was worth it because the highway was in such great shape." Roger loved to drive and was gifted at remembering and documenting the details of his experiences.

Diane also told me about the time Roger wanted to see a live space shuttle launch. Years ago, he, his brother

Gerry, and Gerry's son took a road trip from Pennsylvania to Florida. After the long drive, Gerry and Roger's nephew spent the night before the scheduled launch in a comfortable hotel room. Roger, being parsimonious (i.e., frugal), did not want to pay for a room so he spent the night in a chaise lounge chair by the hotel pool. Unfortunately, fire ants treated Roger like an all-night buffet and he was miserable as a result. To add insult to injury, the launch was scrubbed and they had to get back to Pennsylvania, so they never did experience a launch. From what I understand, the ride home was not their finest hour.

After Diane and I were married and living in our first home in New Jersey, Roger couldn't wait for opportunities to visit. Although he lived approximately three hours from us, he gladly made the long trip. Later, when we moved to a new home in Pennsylvania for my job, Roger's commute was cut down two hours. As usual, he always looked for an excuse to visit. I travelled quite a bit for work during my careers, so visits from Diane's parents were always appreciated. I never liked being away from my family but, knowing that Roger and Vera were with Diane and the kids, gave me great comfort.

And we loved visiting them as well. I enjoyed exploring the small town where they lived and imagined what it was like for Diane to grow up there. Diane's childhood home was in a neighborhood on the top of a mountain. I would accompany Roger to the attic window which offered a spectacular view of the mountain range and valley below. He explained the history of coal mining in the area and where things stood in current times. When the kids were younger, we would walk a few blocks up a hill to a genuine penny candy store. It was like going back in time when life seemed much simpler.

Roger would go all out to decorate his house at Christmastime, just for us! He set up an elaborate wooden platform with miniature homes, lights, landscaping, and of course, a running model train. The kids loved it and looked forward to the visit each year. Full disclosure, I loved it too! I look back at these times with great joy and a bit of sadness that this season is gone.

Each year when we visited my in-laws during the Christmas season, we would travel to the local mall which was beautifully decorated for the holidays. We loved the joyous atmosphere and pictures of the kids with Santa. It was a fun tradition for my family. Interestingly, my father-in-law had participated in the original construction of that mall. In my way of thinking, a part of him was in there! Being a carpenter, he proudly showed us the sections of the mall which he had helped to construct. I didn't know it at the time, but during construction, Roger actually discreetly carved Diane's initials under a bench in a department store dressing room! I'm not sure if anyone ever saw the inscription except for Diane and her parents.

Over the years, stores began to close and the mall became a remnant of its former self. I was saddened when the mall shut down and was eventually razed. Although the mall was just a "thing," I cherished the memories and longed for those days. I know it sounds strange but, when the mall was torn down, it felt like a part of me, or at least our memories went down in the rubble as well.

As a birthday gift one year, Roger did something no one had ever done for me before. He bought me a guitar. Typically, selecting a musical instrument is quite personal. For me personally, I go through a very methodical, well thought-out process and usually like to play the instrument myself in the music store, to get a feel for it before I buy. I don't even look at the price tag until I've found an instrument that suits me well.

Having said all of that, Roger took the risk and went to a local music store where he spoke with a guitar expert. The salesman asked a few questions about my playing habits and consequently recommended a specific instrument. And guess what, he nailed it! He surprised me with a guitar that I likely would have selected if I had visited that music store myself. The acoustic guitar, which I still own and enjoy playing, has a beautiful look and sound. This bold, thoughtful gesture is representative of the love and care he had for me. He always made me feel like a son.

Roger especially enjoyed our houses. When he wasn't visiting us, he was making plans for improvements and upgrades to our homes. He loved using his carpentry and technical skills and I learned so much watching and helping him. He designed and installed intricate doorframes on both our New Jersey and Pennsylvania homes. He also enhanced a crawl space entrance on our first house and built a beautiful corner china closet which we still display proudly. He also built huge, detailed, beautiful doll houses for my two oldest daughters. Sadly, he never had the opportunity to build one for my youngest because he passed away a few months after she was born.

Roger also built an elaborate workbench for me which I still use in my garage. Being the generous person he was, he created a workbench which was nicer and more elaborate than his own, and he was a carpenter! He also built beautiful cases for my electric drill and power saw. There is so much of Roger's influence around our home and I gratefully think of him every time I see or use these items.

When Roger had an idea in mind, he would send his hand-drawn plans in a letter. He was always thinking of little jobs to do around the house. When I would express that I "felt guilty" for him doing so much free work for us, his responses were clear that he lived for doing these things. Looking back, I believe that these jobs gave Roger purpose and a way to show love to us.

In the treasure box I found a detailed, handwritten depiction of how electricity works in the home. Roger laid this all out for my benefit. He had installed several lights and outlets around the house and wanted me to understand how it all worked. To be clear, I still don't understand it and would never attempt to do anything electrical, except installing a doorbell or changing a lightbulb. (I can almost hear you now: "Bob, saying those things are 'electrical' is like calling yourself a chef because you know how to make toast!") But seriously, he was such a great teacher and wanted to impart as much knowledge to me as possible.

Roger knew that I beat myself up for not "being handy" when I was younger. It's a label I wore as a child so I often didn't even try to fix or build anything around the house. Roger didn't see me that way and refused to apply that label to me. He was patient and loved to teach me in a way I could understand. He said continually, "I wish that I could take everything in my head and transfer it to you, Bob."

Don't get me wrong; I can't do anything fancy and never mess with electrical or plumbing, but I have confidence to do other simple jobs I never thought I could. I have built and fixed things around my home, my parents', and my daughters' houses. When I hit a roadblock and can't immediately figure out a solution, I recall what Roger would do. He would improvise and say, "There's always a way to do this." For this reason, I don't give up. That is a credit to my late friend and father-in-law, and I think he would be proud.

It's not in the treasure box, but I distinctly remember a note Roger wrote to me sometime during the twelve years I was blessed to know him. He wanted me to know about his military service in the Philippines as well as different jobs he had held over the years. He served our country proudly and used his carpentry and construction skills to the benefit of our country. His note was a detailed history of his wonderful life.

Roger and Vera were the best in-laws I could have asked for. They loved me like a son and I felt like I had been blessed with a second set of parents. Roger was like a second dad to me and I felt like he was gone much too soon. I am so grateful that they spent so much time with us on extended visits to our homes. And I miss the visits we made to their humble home in a small town I would have been happy to have grown up in. The letters are indeed a treasure, a memorial to happy times and memories.

I'll close this chapter with the most touching, tear-inducing letter I found in the box. Diane had forgotten about this and had tears as well.

The note was from Christmastime. I don't know which year this was, but the letter is gold:

Dear Diane and Bob,

If we were to give you both our love as a Christmas present, the box would not fit in your car nor in your home. So we found other gifts for you both and we will give you a piece of our love each time we meet.

Merry Christmas

    Love,

    Pop

Looking forward to seeing you both for Christmas xxoo

One who has unreliable friends soon comes to ruin, but there is a friend who sticks closer than a brother.
Proverbs 18:24

My Letter to Roger and Vera

Dear Roger and Vera,

While you are no longer with us physically, you remain in my heart and thoughts forever. Our time together on earth was much too short, but I am grateful that we packed so much love and many memories into those years. God could not have provided more perfect in-laws than you!

Thank you for allowing me the privilege and blessing of spending my life with your precious only daughter. It is a trust that I guard with my life and never take for granted. And thank you for all of the visits and help you provided my family when I was away on many business trips. I would give anything to have one of those visits now. Your kindness, love, listening ears, and faith are treasures that are stored up in heaven. I can't wait to see you again, in the presence of our Lord and Savior, Jesus Christ.

Your loving son-in-law (I feel more like a son to you),

Bob

The two letters following were cherished memories. The first, the aforementioned Christmas note that made both of us cry (note that Roger was "Pop" to Diane). The second, one of Roger's letters with home improvement plans. Diane and I had been married for less than a year and were in our first home, in central New Jersey.

> Dear Diane + Bob,
>
> If we were to give you both our love as a Christmas present, the box would not fit in your car nor in your home. So we found other gifts for you both and we will give you a piece of our love each time we meet.
>
> Merry Christmas
> Love
> Pop
>
> looking forward to seeing you both for Christmas.
>
> XX oo

Aug 19, 95

Hi Bob & Diane,

How about this, a letter from Pop. Yea. I have time and ambition to write since I'm on vacation. I also want to do jobs around your house to make things easy for you both. Such as the entrance to your crawl space.

SIDING WALL

OLD DOOR

METAL LID

SIDING

Ground

BLOCK WALL

NEW

GORDON $159
Reg. $169 - Steel
CELLAR DOOR
49"x63"x22". Replace old, worn out wood door. CD-2.

ground

SIDING

DOUBLE DOORS

Chapter 5: Letters from Grandmom

Dear friends, let us love one another, for love comes from God. Everyone who loves has been born of God and knows God.

1 John 4:7

GRANDMOM JONES, MY DAD'S PRECIOUS MOTHER, WENT HOME TO BE WITH THE LORD IN LATE 2014. I had totally forgotten that she had written letters to me. It was a blessing to rediscover these gems.

Grandmom was blessed to live a long life and had a sharp mind until the end. Even when her eyesight deteriorated, she still read books because she had a passion for them. I don't ever remember her without a smile. Well, maybe once, and I'll tell you about that in a moment!

I only have four letters from Grandmom, dated 1996 through 2004, but each one is special. As I read her letters, I found myself once more so thankful for these treasures which have provided priceless memories of my loved ones. Like other relatives, I know that Grandmom also sent cards for birthdays and special occasions. Those cards are buried somewhere in our basement and perhaps I'll search (or better yet, ask Diane to search, as I would need a map to navigate) for those when I finish writing this book.

Grandmom had amazing penmanship as reflected in very neat cursive writing in her letters. I think that my dad picked up her skill to write neatly. My parents, siblings, and close relatives referred to me as "Robbie" growing up. Grandmom always wrote my name as "Robby" but I never brought this to her attention. I kind of liked the variation and it was just a unique thing between us, so I never saw a need to change it.

I only remember one time when I saw Grandmom upset. One summer day Grandpop Jones picked me up at our home for a trip to north Philadelphia. It's one of the few times I remember doing a grandson-grandfather thing with him. On this venture, Grandpop wanted to check out a sporting goods store outside of the city. On our way back, driving through center city Philadelphia, Grandpop did not notice the red light at a busy intersection. As the light changed, he proceeded through. I was sitting in the passenger seat, not wearing a seatbelt. Back then I'm pretty sure that mandatory seatbelt laws were not in effect. Moreover, I am not certain that Grandpop's car was even equipped with them! Most people I knew did not think to use seatbelts at that time. Personally, I'm thankful for the emphasis on safety today!

As we came into the intersection, I could see the stream of cars, two-lanes worth, coming at us as their traffic signal had just turned green. I knew we were going to be hit, I just didn't know exactly where or how. The first car to come through had no chance to avoid us and he plowed into the ride side of Grandpop's car, jerking me forward into the dashboard.

Thankfully, aside from my sore forearm and wrist, no one else was hurt, though the experience really shook me. The guy who hit us was nice enough. He could have been angry as the accident was not his fault. After exchanging insurance information, we proceeded across the Ben Franklin Bridge to New Jersey. Anytime Grandpop hit a bump or made a right turn, the fender would rub against the front right tire, making a screeching noise. When Grandpop stopped at his house to show the damage to Grandmom, she was not happy. She never spoke a word but the expression on her face said it all. That was the only time I've ever seen her upset!

As I read through Grandmom's letters, I was struck by the fact that she found time to write me letters, in addition to the cards I mentioned. Dad had six siblings, one of whom (a sister) died at birth. Therefore, Grandmom had a number of grand and great-grandchildren. I'm not sure that I know the "grand" total and I've never been good at math anyway! The point is, Grandmom had to spread her love and affection out among many family members. I have no idea how she found time to give attention to every precious soul, but she did. It was obvious from her letters that she deeply loved and was proud of each of her grand and great-grandchildren.

When I was a teenager, before I was old enough to drive, I won tickets to see a famous country music artist who was performing at a local venue. Mom and Dad couldn't go and I needed an adult to accompany me. Grandmom agreed to go to the concert with me and we had an enjoyable evening. Again, this made me feel special given the number of grandchildren she had!

In October of 1996, Grandmom wrote a nice two-and-a-half-page letter to my family. Her continually positive perspective was still evident in her words, "I am getting along as well as expected for an old lady, you know, a few aches and pains but I try to put it behind me and keep on going each day." I was also comforted by her faith. She wrote in the same letter: "I love you all and keep you in my prayers." Reading that now gave me a renewed glimpse into her compassionate heart.

In August of 1999, Grandmom wrote and thanked me for visiting her in the hospital. I vaguely remember the visit but her words really touched me as I read them again: "Rob, I want to take this time to thank you again for calling and making the visit to the hospital to see me, you made me very happy and proud of you." I might be in the second half of life but felt just like a little grandson again as I read her precious words.

I was so thankful that I got to take Mom and Dad to see Grandmom months before she passed away. This was two years before dad's second stroke so he was able to drive to my home from southern Virginia. I then drove them both to New Jersey for the visit. Dad had not seen his mother or sister for many years. It was such a blessing to watch them love on each other and reminisce about their lives. They talked, looked at old pictures and newspaper clippings, and laughed. It was like no time had passed between them.

At Grandmom's funeral, I was able to reconnect with aunts, uncles, and cousins I had not seen in many years. Her life blessed each of us in special ways. It's only been a little over six years since she has been gone, but her impact will live on, with me and her remaining family members.

I thank God for these letters, treasures which were written with tenderness and love. Treasures which will live on, stored up in heaven.

Children's children are a crown to the aged, and parents are the pride of their children.
Proverbs 17:6

My Letter to Grandmom

Dear Grandmom,

As I read through the letters you took time to write me, so many wonderful memories flashed through my mind. The visits, the conversations, and the laughs are still fresh in my mind. Thank you for your love and the time you took for me, Diane, and my children. We were blessed to have you for so long in our lives. Your faith is evident from the way you lived your life and the precious words in your letters.

I am so thankful that I had the opportunity to visit and spend time with you before you went home to be with Jesus. I can't wait for the heavenly reunion where I can see you again!

Love always,

Robby

Grandmom wrote this letter on August 9, 1997. Notice how she referred to me as "Robby." Also notice the impeccable penmanship!

> Dear Robby + Diane + Girls
>
> Received your most welcome letter, very happy to hear from you. Rob, I want to take this time to thank you again for calling and making the visit to the hospital to see me, you made me very happy and proud of of you. I am praying you have a safe trip.
>
> I am feeling much better but on Aug 22nd I have to go for a one more test, after that maybe I will be able to relax and get on me two feet again.
>
> I was very sorry I couldn't attend the family reunion but I will try to be at the next one, if God see fit, I hope so it would be nice to see all of you again.
>
> Diane please send me the birthday dates of the two last little ones and their names so I can keep it touch with them.
>
> I will close for now, take care and keep it touch (ours)
>
> Love to all
> Grand Mom +
> Great Grand Mom

Chapter 6: Letters from Pop

For no one can lay any foundation other than the one already laid, which is Jesus Christ.

1 Corinthians 3:11

My desire to find and read Pop's letters was the main reason I started to write this book. In fact, I had originally considered, "Letters from Pop," as the title. My expectation was to locate his letters, read through them, and document the stories and blessings contained therein. But that was before I knew about the treasure chest and its precious contents. That was before I understood the legacy he had inspired.

Before opening the treasure chest, I was already confident that Pop had written a significant number of letters. However, the size of the stack surprised me and was even thicker than I imagined! He had written me more letters than anyone else. Pop literally wrote me hundreds of pages of letters. It really is incredible when I look at the sheer number of letters he penned. I am still in awe when I think about how much time it must have taken him to sit down and pen these letters which average four pages each.

After reading his letters again, I'm convinced that I did not fully appreciate the contents until recently. They are filled with love, and rich in history, some of which I was not aware of until now. Moreover, I don't know if it was the busyness of my career, raising a family, or just my poor memory, but I felt like I was reading his letters for the first time. While I regret not having paid better attention back then, I am also eternally grateful that I have his letters as a record of Pop's humble but amazing life; a life that continues to impact my journey today. His influence on my life really cannot be overstated.

To know Pop was to love him. And so, I will provide a little background and some rich stories so that you, too, may gain just a small glimpse of the legacy that he left.

Pop's History

Pop had tough, very humble beginnings but you would have never known it if you talked to him. He never complained. Born in Alabama, Pop did not have his parents around for long. His mother died when he was only seven years old. His father died when he was eleven, leaving him as an orphan. Pop and his two sisters were sent to live with different relatives and others who graciously took them in. Amazingly, his sisters were not reunited again until they were adults! Pop lived with a priest for a short time until an uncle secured a job for him with the railroad. Pop was only thirteen at the time!

When he was sixteen, he relocated to New Jersey to live with an uncle who had a plumbing business. Despite being an orphan with only an eighth-grade education, Pop managed to support himself from the time he was a teenager through the rest of his life. Many, including myself, don't realize how blessed we are in this country, at this time in history. While I've faced some trials in my life, they pale in comparison to the things Pop endured.

In one of Pop's first letters to me in 1983, he talked about his time in the Army. Pop proudly served in Panama, as a main gate guard at what was then Fort Amador. Just after he had joined the Army and was about to leave for Panama, Pop met Nana at a roller-skating rink in New Jersey. They had a four-year, long-distance courtship, and married once Pop was discharged. Sweetly, they both wrote to each other continually. But the fact that he was single at the time he was serving, did not sink in until now. He spent the better part of three years in Panama, and said in his letter to me that he checked the mail every day. Whenever he received a letter from home it lifted his spirits. Now I understand why Pop couldn't wait to receive mail from home. The letters kept him going! Nana was his soulmate and they were totally devoted to each other for almost sixty years of marriage. Pop was thirty-two years old when he was honorably discharged at the Brooklyn Army base in New York and went home to marry my grandmother.

He and Nana, like my immediate family, lived in southern New Jersey, across the river from Philadelphia. In fact, on most days, commercial airplanes would fly directly over their house on approach to the international airport in Philadelphia. The planes flew so low that you could clearly see the airline insignia, windows, and wheels down. One time a pilot waved to me as he was landing. Okay, I made that last part up but that is how close we lived to the city!

Nana and Pop lived in the same New Jersey home for fifty-eight years. Her father had built the home in 1902 and Nana herself had lived in that same home for more than seventy-five years! My great uncle Fred, Nana's brother, also lived with them until he passed away in the early 1990s. Based on Pop's letters, they loved living there. I have such great memories of my childhood at that home; playing in the yard, eating meals, admiring Pop's massive, amazing garden, and picking vegetables from it. It was the only home they knew but the time would eventually come when it would get to be too much.

Pop's Been Working on the Railroad

Pop worked for many years on the railroad. He was a conductor on the line from Philadelphia to Chestnut Hill. He had also worked on the trolley system in Philadelphia, right after he and Nana married. I remember those years vividly. I won't get into too much detail about his career because, frankly, I don't know a whole lot. My younger brother has actually done extensive research on Pop's history with the railroad and knows much more than I do. My brother shares Pop's interest in trains, both the real ones and model trains. That said, I will share a few memories as well as nuggets Pop shared in his letters.

I remember numerous visits to my grandparents' home during the years when Pop was working for the railroad. After dinners, Pop would sit at his little desk in the dining room and do what he called, "book work." I never understood what he was doing, but he had a collection of small punched tickets that he used to mark seats of passengers on the train who had paid their fares. We weren't allowed to touch those tickets but often Pop would give the kids blank ones as souvenirs and to keep us occupied while he worked!

I also distinctly recall the day Pop retired from the railroad. Nana, my parents, and my siblings went on his final train ride from Philly to Chestnut Hill, where his colleagues held a retirement party. The engineer allowed us kids to ride up front where he operated the commuter train. This memory is still so clear in my mind and it was a wonderful experience.

In a letter from 1996, the year before Pop went home to be with the Lord, he talked about his commute to Chestnut Hill with the railroad. He wrote that he got up at 4:00 a.m. and left the house at 5:30. He also wrote in that letter, "I would give anything to be ten years younger." *Sometimes I feel that way as well!*

Pop, always fascinated by weather phenomena, discussed a big snowstorm which hit the area. I'm guessing that the letter was likely written in 1993 when a massive blizzard hit the east coast. Pop wrote that he hadn't seen that much snow since the 1930s. He reported that he couldn't get home for two days back then; thirty or forty trolley cars were tied up for two or three blocks and could not move due to the weather. Workers had to chip ice from the rails and overhead wires to get the trolley cars going again. I can't imagine what that would have been like!

In addition to the railroad, Pop was an experienced wallpaper hanger and auto mechanic. He was laid off several times from the railroad and supported Nana and my mom by doing odd jobs, including wallpapering and working at a local service station as a mechanic. I accompanied Pop to several jobs where he taught me how to hang wallpaper, perhaps also a lost art these days.

My brother also shares Pop's love and talent for fixing cars and is very skilled in the field of auto mechanics. I, on the other hand, need a trained mechanic for just about everything! Pop taught me the importance of regular oil changes. He would say, "Rob, oil is the life of the car." This advice stuck with me and I ensure that my vehicles get regular check-ups and oil changes. Pop was a whiz with older model cars but wrote about how costly and complex cars had become with the advent of more electronics.

While my memories of Pop are centered on his thirty years on the railroad, as a wallpaper hanger, and auto mechanic, Mom recently furnished me a list of all of the jobs he worked over the years. The impressive list of over sixteen careers includes work as a truck driver, shipfitter, plumber and pipe-fitter's helper, and laborer at a number of companies in the Philadelphia area. He even sold fruit and vegetables from a truck during the Great Depression; anything to support himself and his family. It was truly amazing considering his humble beginnings and education! I admired his life but didn't fully appreciate it until I was older.

Pop's Garden & Hobbies

Pop maintained the ultimate vegetable garden. I wish that I had pictures to share, but, take my word, it was large and impressive. The garden consisted of rows of every kind of plant, from his locally-famous tomatoes, to peppers, lima and green beans, carrots, corn, beets, cucumbers, eggplant, radishes, even parsley! He wrote that some tomatoes he grew in the early days weighed almost four pounds! I really don't know how he managed to maintain it every spring and summer with a full-time job and everything else he had going on. As a kid, I would get lost in that garden!

Reading through his letters again, I learned some other things I did not know.

First, Pop told a story from when he was about eleven, before his dad died at age thirty-eight from a burst appendix. Pop's father had a sixty-acre farm which he somehow balanced with work at the shipyard, and Pop worked on the farm when he was a boy. Pop said they had chickens, turkeys, cows, a horse, and a goat on the farm. After reading that account, I can see why Pop loved gardening and he understood the commitment and work that went into farming.

Second, Pop planted seeds in his attic as early as February each year. That's where and when he would start a number of his plants. In a letter from early 1984, Pop wrote that he had ordered seeds from a catalog and planted them in his attic on February 15th. He had his own formula for planting, including how deep to dig holes, how much and frequently to water, and the application of cow manure which evidently was a key to healthy plants. In that same letter, while I was living in Texas, Pop wrote: "It is quite a job but I enjoy the efforts I put into the garden. I like to see what I can grow." I love that he enjoyed his hobby so much and admired the tireless effort he put into it. His labor of love paid dividends every summer.

Pop also wrote how much my great Uncle Fred helped around the house and garden. I was reminded that, in addition to Pop's vegetable garden, he and Uncle Fred had a beautiful rose garden as well. I also recalled that Pop and Uncle Fred had maintained apple and pear trees in the yard, and they yielded delicious fruit each year!

I must mention one quick side note about Pop and Uncle Fred, something my mom reminded me of recently. Pop demonstrated a love for Uncle Fred, his brother-in-law, that is not often seen today. Uncle Fred lived with Nana and Pop until the day he went home to be with the Lord. When Uncle Fred's health declined and he needed personal care, Pop took care of things. I won't get into the details, but imagine the emotional work, love, and trust that go into bathing and feeding a loved one. Pop never complained. He told mom, "God gave us jobs to do, even if sometimes they aren't pleasant." He was a consummate gentleman.

In one of Pop's letters from the late 1980s, he indicated that he reduced the size of his garden to 50%. It had become too much to take care of, especially when Uncle Fred's health declined. At that time, Pop graciously allowed his pastor to plant and use the other half of the garden as he saw fit. He was such a generous man and always looked for opportunities to bless others! Pop really lived out Philippians 2:3, "Do nothing out of selfish ambition or vain conceit. Rather, in humility value others above yourselves."

Pop had so many interests but lived a very simple life. When Pop retired from the railroad, he took up a unique hobby in addition to gardening: he made jewelry boxes in a small attic work area. Amazingly enough, as I was finishing this book, I located a jewelry box Pop had made for one of my girls. It was sitting in the room where my youngest daughter grew up, and I noticed it as I wrote this very chapter! It's amazing how things become familiar to us and we look past obvious treasures. This box has been sitting on that dresser for years and it just now caught my attention.

Pop made the rectangular box itself out of wood. However, the only visible wood (painted white) is on the bottom and on the four carefully-carved feet. The top has two hinges in the back and a clasp on the front which allows the box to be closed. The inside is carefully covered in green felt. The box is quite an exquisite piece of workmanship from my gifted Pop! I can't imagine how long it took him to make one. He made a variety of sizes. And the best part: the entire box is covered with actual seashells which are adhered to the surface! I know that Pop collected shells at the beach but he also bought some from specialty stores. He had bags of shells in his attic! I can't count them all but there must be at least 100, unique and perfect seashells on this box. The craftsmanship and love that went into it is evident. And he made many of them which could have fetched a great deal of money, but he gave them as gifts to bless others.

Me and Pop

I spent a great deal of time with Pop when I was younger but, in general, my knowledge of his life was limited to what I observed. Mom told me things about Pop's history over the years but I did not retain much of the details. Maybe I wasn't the best listener or perhaps it's just the way I'm wired. My wife, on the other hand, remembers everything. That can be a blessing and a curse, but it's *mostly a blessing*!

We called him "Pop-Pop" growing up but somewhere along the line the name was shortened. I don't know why and can't recall exactly when. Perhaps it was a good name when we were kids but the shortened name was more suited to adults? He did call himself "Pop-Pop" when he spoke to his great grandchildren. But he referred to himself as "Pop" in the letters. Until the day he passed away, he referred to me as "Robbie" or "Rob," the nickname my family gave to me. They are the only ones who call me by that name.

I grew up in a time where families lived in close proximity to each other. Grandmom and Grandpop Jones, Dad's parents, lived about twenty minutes away in a city neighborhood and we visited them every so often. They had six children and a number of grandchildren, so visits were staggered to accommodate everyone.

Nana and Pop, Mom's parents, were only a ten-minute drive from home and we had frequent visits and meals at their house. Mom was an only child, so us kids had Nana and Pop's full attention as grandparents. I have wonderful memories of holidays together, trips to the shore, and adventures to New York City. Back in the day, a ferry ride to the Statue of Liberty was easy and I remember going up into the structure twice as a kid! And of course, I was always in awe of Pop's garden.

Since we were so close to Philly it stands to reason that we followed the professional sports teams there. Pop was a casual football fan but he especially enjoyed following the Phillies baseball team. I recall that every Sunday in the summer he would have his television tuned to the afternoon game. Pop had a console TV with an antenna so he only picked up local stations. He did not have cable installed at the house and never wanted it. Most home games, except for Sundays, were only available on cable TV. For this reason, he would listen to non-televised games on a small transistor radio.

While my dad and I went to a number of live games over the years, Pop didn't attend one until I was a teenager. The Phils were playing one Sunday at the Vet (the old Veterans Stadium) and Dad bought tickets for himself, me, and Pop. It took some convincing but Pop finally agreed to go the game. I was so excited for him! He was such a fan of baseball but had never experienced the excitement of actually being there for a live game. During this particular game, we were sitting behind home plate, in what I considered really good seats, and Pop watched intently. As the first player from the opposing team came to bat, Pop, always with a great sense of humor, exclaims, "He swings like an old rusty gate!" Pop was kidding around, but I still smile when I think about this. He always had these funny little sayings that he would recite on cue. I can still hear his voice saying these things.

Pop also loved restaurants and his sense of humor surfaced there as well. Each year, just after Christmas, my dad would load up the Ford LTD station wagon with Mom, the kids, Nana, and Pop. I think with seven of us packed into the car, there wasn't room for an onion-skin letter. We would travel about forty-five minutes to a fancy restaurant outside of Atlantic City. This became a tradition and we all looked forward to it. The fare consisted of several courses which always prompted Dad to say at the end of the meal, "If any of you goes home hungry, it's your own fault." He was right; the meal and the experience were wonderful. And without fail, when coffee and dessert came, Pop would take a sip of the coffee, smile and say, "This coffee tastes like it came from an old boot," even though the drink was delicious. His sense of humor and continuous upbeat personality always brought a smile to my face.

I distinctly remember one year when Nana and Pop arrived at the house for our annual trek to the restaurant. As we piled into our station wagon, Dad assumed that everyone was safely seated so he pulled away from the curb. Unfortunately, Pop was halfway into the back seat, with one leg in the car and one out the open door, positioned on the curb. I am not making this up! As Pop hopped on one foot for a few seconds I remember yelling,

"Dad, stop! Pop isn't completely in!" Dad quickly stopped the car. Fortunately, Pop was not hurt and we got a good laugh out of it. Pop was such a gentleman, he probably would have tried to hop all the way to Atlantic City if he could, just so he didn't cause a fuss! I have no idea why I remember things like this but the letters brought back these precious memories as well.

I also recall annual trips to Wildwood where Nana and Pop would drive the kids to the shore for an evening on the boardwalk. The routine was always the same each summer. We would leave in the early afternoon and stop at a restaurant near the beach for a turkey dinner. Nana and Pop loved going out to restaurants. Pop wrote quite a bit about how much he loved to eat at buffets, especially after he moved to Virginia. In one letter he wrote, "I never saw such a variety of food, all one could eat for the low price of $5.99!" Pop also loved to walk around malls with Nana and he wrote about that in his letters. He loved his routines and enjoyed life to the fullest.

On these annual trips, we would head to the boardwalk in Wildwood, New Jersey after dinner to enjoy the rides and games. Pop would give us each a little money, back when the prices were reasonable, to ride the log flume or walk through the haunted house. We also occasionally won a stuffed animal or small trinket by mastering a game of skill on the boardwalk. We would get home later in the evening, exhausted but grateful for the fun day with our grandparents.

Pop was a character; I don't think that he read music but he loved to play the harmonica and noodle around on a small guitar he had purchased. On the way to the shore, Pop would sometimes whip the harmonica out and start playing it *while he was driving*, but only on deserted roads where there was no traffic. This always prompted a response from Nana such as, "Will you put that thing away and keep your eyes on the road!" It is wonderful to recall these memories and I am so grateful that I inherited Pop's guitar and have it in my possession.

In my career, I travelled all over the world for business. Whenever I came to a destination I'd never been to, if I were there for a week or two, I would send a postcard to my wife and children. I also sent postcards to my parents, in-laws, and grandparents. It made me feel connected to home and the family enjoyed hearing about my adventures. Pop referred to some of the postcards I had sent him in his letters back to me. He always loved to hear from me. I also found postcards from a few of their Florida trips.

One other thing my dear mother mentioned, and I had forgotten about this as well: Somewhere along the line, Pop became known as "the candy man." He earned this moniker in the New Jersey church he and Nana attended.

Pop got into the habit of carrying pieces of candy in his pocket and he would hand treats to children in the congregation. Needless to say, he was popular with the kids; they flocked to him when he entered the church!

The Decision to Relocate

As we all will, both Pop and Nana experienced the reality that our bodies age. The Bible tells us as much in 2 Corinthians 4:16 where it says, "Therefore we do not lose heart. Though outwardly we are wasting away, yet inwardly we are being renewed day by day." I am grateful that inwardly the Lord Jesus Christ does renew His followers, day by day. I am the living proof of His transforming power, which I don't deserve. But outwardly? Yes, I'm feeling what is stated in this verse. There are things I used to do that would be difficult now. Sometimes I forget my age and pay the price after doing something I shouldn't!

As stated earlier, my grandparents lived in the house that Nana's dad had built in the early 1900s. It was a stately two-story dwelling with a full attic and basement. To me, that's really a four-story house; it was quite the effort to ascend all of the steps from the basement to the attic.

As the years progressed, climbing up and down stairs became increasingly difficult for my grandparents. After my parents moved to Virginia it became harder for Nana and Pop to manage the home, and Mom and Dad were not nearby to assist. My younger brother, who lived in the area, was a big help to my grandparents, but it became difficult for him to visit often since he had a career and family of his own. He also lived a distance away from Nana and Pop.

Pop's letters in the early 1990s indicated that my parents wanted Nana and him to move to Virginia. Dad had a large piece of land and offered to have a house built on the same property for Nana and Pop. Sometime in the early 1990s Pop wrote this in a letter to me: "Your dad wants us to sell and move to Virginia. Nana isn't ready yet." In a subsequent letter Pop wrote, "Nana and I haven't ruled out the possibility of moving to Virginia. We may have to…"

Things got to a point where my grandparents had no choice. In 1995, they placed their house on the market and it sold. I can't imagine how hard it was the day they made the decision to sell the only home Nana ever knew, the home where Pop lived for his entire marriage, and the home where my mother was raised. They also trusted my dad to orchestrate the construction of their new home in Virginia. To this day I can't fathom the thought process and leap of faith it took for them to make this difficult decision.

Pop's letter from 1995 summarized the day they moved:

> "Your mom, dad, brother, and neighbors loaded the truck. I (Pop) had planted tomatoes and other crops but we moved before we could harvest. The neighbors were the beneficiaries."

Based on a letter from Pop, after the move, he also stated that the neighborhood gave them a going-away party. They left New Jersey at 2:30 in the afternoon and arrived at their new home in southern Virginia at 10:30 p.m. Pop concluded that letter with the statement that "they have adjusted to Virginia and like it very much."

Pop made the most of his short time in Virginia. He wrote that he had started a garden at the new place. Even though the soil was hard and red, Pop was able to plant and successfully raise forty tomato plants, lima beans, string beans, corn, peppers, cucumbers, beets, and lettuce! He also remarked how hard my dad worked on his little farm, while holding down a full-time job and taking care of Nana and Pop. Pop understood the commitment of maintaining farm animals and wrote, "I don't know how your dad does it, there is very little time for amusement."

A lot of change came during those years for all of us. In 1995, our youngest daughter was born and Nana and Pop moved in April. Then my dear father-in-law passed away in August. Pop enjoyed the remainder of 1995 and 1996 at his new home but sadly passed away on January 7, 1997. Nana lived for several more years in Virginia and went home to be with the Lord on November 7, 2001.

I recall two additional memories which warm my heart.

First, Nana and Pop brought their console television set from New Jersey to Virginia. Like always, Pop did not have cable and refused to get it even after he moved. He relied on an antenna for reception of local stations and he was content with that. What an example he set for me and it reminds me of the Scripture from 1 Timothy 6:6, "But godliness with contentment is great gain."

Lastly, I can still hear his voice when I think of the times when I would call him in Virginia. The conversation would start this way:

> *"Hi Pop, it's Rob."*
>
> *"Hello Rob."*
>
> *"How are you doing, Pop?"*
>
> *"Oh, pretty good for an old gent..."*

He would say he was "pretty good" even when he had declining health. He always looked at the positives in life!

His Writing

Pop started writing to me as soon as I moved to Texas in 1983. He loved to write letters and it showed. He never dated his letters so exact timeframes were difficult to discern. However, the contents of the letters contain clues which gave me a general idea of the year. As I read through his letters again, I learned that Pop was writing letters long before I was born.

Pop wrote about everything and anything in his letters to me. It would take several books if I dissected the details of every letter.

As I progressed with my reading of Pop's letters, I noticed a few common threads:

First, Pop typically wrote in blue pen and in cursive! I wonder how many folks write in cursive today? I personally avoid writing in cursive because of my penmanship. Every once in a while, Pop must have run out of ink because a few letters were written with a combination of blue and black ink. Second, most of the time he wrote his letters on 5 ½ x 8 ½ paper. He only deviated and wrote on larger paper a few times. Thirdly, he always numbered the pages with roman numerals. In most of his letters, Pop talked first about his health and the weather. It was almost like an extension of the salutation. In his later letters he would actually write the current temperature in the upper right-hand corner of the first page. Random stuff, I know, but fascinating to me! Oh, and I think Pop may have pioneered the predecessor to the term "LOL" because when he made a joke in his letters, he followed his remarks with the word, "Ha."

Pop often wrote about how blessed he was whenever my brother, sister, and their families visited. He took the time to write out stories and current events he had read in the newspaper. Interestingly, some of the same issues today existed back then, and Pop mentioned a few of them. Pop had his political opinions like most people, but he was always humble about them, never divisive. He sent an article on the partisanship regarding a proposed raising of the federal minimum wage. He also wrote about budget issues in nearby towns. There really is nothing new under the sun!

After Diane and I were married, Pop and Nana always passed on their love to Diane's parents in the letters. They loved each of their great-grandchildren dearly and always referred to my girls as "little dolls."

Pop wrote about the time he was hospitalized and I came to visit with my oldest and middle daughters. I did not remember this account where he evidently offered my middle daughter a cookie but she was sheepish and would not take it from him. From what I can ascertain from the letter, she was only a few years old at the time. As the story goes, Pop eventually gave the cookie to my oldest daughter and she passed it to my middle daughter who gladly accepted. Another wonderful memory!

One of the first letters I received in Texas came from my great Uncle Fred who lived with them as I mentioned earlier. I think it was the only one he ever wrote me, but it was special.

Uncle Fred was an introspective, sagacious man, and he always offered words of wisdom. I felt like whenever I visited my grandparents' home and spoke with Uncle Fred, I was sitting at the feet of an oracle. Significantly, many years later, God used Uncle Fred's death to lead me to Jesus Christ.

Uncle Fred evidently wrote the letter on behalf of Nana and Pop who were on a Florida vacation, a few months after I had moved to Texas. Nana and Pop made several trips to Florida in their lifetime, as Pop wrote, "just to get away and get recharged." He always drove from New Jersey to Florida and never took an airplane. Nana, like Uncle Fred, did not drive a car.

I remember a story of Uncle Fred once falling asleep on the bus after work and missing his stop for home!

Because Uncle Fred would rely on the public bus from southern New Jersey to his workplace in the city, I'm sure he was tired at the end of the work day. I don't recall how far he travelled towards Atlantic City before discovering this, nor how long it took to catch a bus going the other direction.

In his letter dated October 3, 1983, Uncle Fred shared encouragement and insight with me. Since I had just graduated college and was starting out in my career, his words in the letter really motivated me. He asserted that the opportunities in the 1980s were greater than in the 1930s. This was interesting to me and must have given me pause back then, because jobs were extremely difficult to find when I graduated college. But his remarks gave me perspective; compared to the 30s, I realized things really weren't so bad when I graduated. He was all about hard work and personal responsibility, which are Biblical virtues. He stated in the letter, "Get an education, the rest is up to you." Given the dire economic times in which he grew up, these were profound words. He did not have a college education but was one of the wisest men I've ever known.

One other thing I noticed: Although Nana did not write letters per se, she often wrote a small note at the end of Pop's. Shortly after I received the aforementioned letter from Uncle Fred, I was pleased to find a letter from Pop in my Texas mailbox. At the bottom of the letter Nana had written, "Here is a small check for you. Thanks for your nice letter when we were in Florida. We enjoyed hearing from you."

Nana was a wonderful cook and I always looked forward to meals at her home. She made amazing dishes of "comfort food" and I especially enjoyed her homemade desserts. Her coconut cake and key lime pie were amazing! She made the best strawberry parfait and rice pudding I have ever tasted. And Nana also made the best sweet tea in the world! We referred to it as "iced tea" when I was growing up. I learned of the term "sweet tea" when I lived in Texas. In fact, restaurant servers taught me that if you just order "tea" in Texas, you get sweet tea.

I don't know how she did it, but Nana's formula of water (which she distilled herself in a machine), a certain number of tea bags, raw sugar, and lemon were the perfect mixture. During my college years, if she knew that I was coming for a visit, she would always have a glass of her perfect tea ready for me. I've had good sweet tea in restaurants but none has ever measured up to hers. And as hard as I've tried, I have never been able to replicate Nana's sweet tea on my own. Maybe because she added a special ingredient of love? I was reminded of this when I read one of Pop's letters from 1983. In it he wrote, "Every time Nana makes tea, she thinks of you, Rob…"

An Unexpected Treasure

God never ceases to amaze me. I started to write this book based on the letters I discovered in the treasure box. When my dear mother learned that I had taken on this initiative she was in the middle of a downsizing project, going through old mementos, articles, cards, and letters. As I was about to finish the draft of this chapter, Mom sent me a text with a screenshot. Her note said, "Did you ever get the attached? I am cleaning old boxes of paper."

I had never seen the document Mom referenced in her text. She had sent me the first page of an article from Nana and Pop's church in New Jersey, the same church I attended as a youth. I believe that the article was included in the church bulletin or a newsletter. From hints within the article, I deduced that it was written in November of 1991. For perspective, Diane and I had been living in Pennsylvania for about two years at that time and were awaiting the birth of our second child.

I read the article eagerly but suspected that there was more to it. Page one ended in the middle of a sentence. I called Mom and asked if there was a second page and, after some searching, she confirmed that there was. Consequently, she sent that to me. I've used this phrase throughout the book but it applies here as well: What I held in my hand was a treasure worth more to me than gold!

This article was written by a man from their church named Paul Rogers. He evidently interviewed Nana and Pop late in 1991 and wrote a beautiful narrative about their life together. It was heartwarming and a colossal blessing to see a non-family member's account of how Pop influenced those around him. I also discovered things about my grandparents which corroborated what I wrote previously in this chapter. However, I also learned several details about them that I did not know until now. The most precious gem in the article was the story of how Nana and Pop came to Jesus Christ.

Before going any further with this treasure, I checked the church's website and contacted its current pastor who informed me that the author is still living. I was able to make e-mail contact with Paul and have gotten to know him, which was an added blessing. He did a wonderful job on the article and I was able to express my gratitude to him directly.

I've edited the article to remove specific names but I'll let the story speak for itself:

UP CLOSE with the CRANDALLS

You may know him as "The Candy Man" and her as his steadfast companion, always by his side on Sunday morning during worship service. Or perhaps you know him as our best candidate from the church to win the coveted world record of the largest Jersey tomato. And you've got to believe his wife is the best cook in our congregation having lived most of her many years with a fine gardener.

The relationship of Olga and Arthur began in 1929 thanks to an ambitious friend of Arthur's who assured him, "I'll get you a girlfriend." As it turned out, this friend had a girlfriend, who had a girlfriend who thought having a boyfriend was a fine idea. Arthur wasn't any kind of roller skater, in fact he didn't skate at all, but a rendezvous with this starlet at the local roller-skating rink sounded just fine. After all, if you're looking for the finest ladies in town you find them at the rink on Saturday night. Olga fortunately had off from work this particular Saturday night and agreed to the whole plan.

Now that all the hard work was done the rest was up to the Good Lord. And He must have thought the whole thing was a good idea, too, because after the nerves calmed down and the sweaty palms passed, Arthur "thought she was swell" and Olga "thought he was great!"

During the next five years our country had some very hard times, but during which there was no shortage of love for Arthur and Olga. And if absence and fondness are related, Arthur's 3 years in Panama helped solidify the inevitable. This month will hail the 54th anniversary of their marriage.

If you happened to have a spare 15 cents in 1932 you could ride the Market Street trolley out to 69th Street and back. Chances are the motor man on your trolley was Arthur. Arthur recalls a later job he had with the Pennsylvania Railroad. Each day included a trip to Toms River with an eight-hour layover. Well that was a fine time for the crew on the train to play some cards or go fishing. A day's catch of blowfish would please Olga. She had a fine recipe for the delicate filet strips.

One day the Tom's River bridge caught fire and the layover was expected to be quite lengthy. This was the perfect chance for Arthur to surprise his wife with some succulent flounder filets. So off to the other side of Barnegat Bay they went.

Unsuspectingly, a storm blew in and the bay kicked up. They were afraid they wouldn't get back in time for the train but a man in a motor boat offered them a ride. Arthur stood in the bow as the boat sped through the high seas. To his surprise a huge wave came across the bow and knocked him over. But those flounder filets were sure worth it!

The Crandall's relationship with the church goes back 7 or 8 years but their relationship with the Lord goes back much further. Olga's mother was Catholic and Arthur "went to all the churches."

One particular evening, before they were married, the course of their lives was to change. Olga's sister invited them to a church in Camden. During an altar call that night they both accepted the Lord into their hearts.

From that point forward they learned to pray and read the Bible. Olga boasts about her favorite Bible verse, Philippians 4:13: "I can do all things in Him Who strengthens me."

The years have been good to Olga and Arthur. Their eyes light up when they mention that their third great grandchild is on the way. And if you ever need advice on how to grow a bigger tomato, just ask Mr. Crandall. After all, his personal record of 3 lbs. 12 oz. is one BIG tomato.

A Legacy Through Letters

Pop's letters are tantamount to a tapestry, a rich piece of art with many intricate facets. His letters encompass a plethora of personal thoughts and history, but above all, immense love. Of humble beginnings and little formal education, he was such an unassuming, gentle, friendly, gifted man. He was also one of the wisest, most hard working, responsible men I've ever known.

Another thing that stood out to me as I revisited these letters was the depth of Pop's faith. Despite Pop's influence when I was younger, I didn't get serious about a relationship with Jesus Christ until the early 1990s, when I was about thirty years old. I must have glossed over some of Pop's words in his letters the first time because I don't remember much of what he wrote about the Lord. But his love for Jesus Christ is woven throughout the letters. He prayed for me daily and included handwritten words to hymns. One of his favorites, and now mine too, was "My Hope is Built on Nothing Less."[1] In fact, sometime in the 1990s he closed one of the letters with the words to that hymn.

Pop wrote that he was grateful when I gave my life to Jesus Christ. He typically closed his letters with this:

---

[1] Edward Mote. "My Hope is Built on Nothing Less." Composed by William B. Bradbury, 1834.

"May the good Lord keep you, excuse this writing, and write when you can…" We wrote back and forth a great deal between 1983 and 1997. I didn't appreciate it as much as I do now.

I'll leave you with two random tidbits which made me smile and chuckle.

First, Pop loved to write about people and their stories. I didn't remember this one, but he wrote this in a letter I received while living in Texas. In it he tells the story about a friend who took a bus trip from New Jersey to California.

He and his wife were away for about a month. When they returned, they discovered that their car had been stolen. The insurance company only agreed to give $600. As Pop stated, "$600 won't buy much!" Interestingly, a week later, the car was located several miles away. The insurance company directed Pop's friend to remove the license plates from the vehicle. The friend removed the plates and then tried to start the car. However, as Pop writes, "the car caught fire and burned up, but he did salvage the license plates." I loved the way Pop looked at life, always an optimist, with a "looking on the bright side" perspective!

Lastly, I have no doubt that I inherited my "corny" sense of humor from Pop. In addition to the "Pop-isms" I shared with you earlier, he would ask things like, "Rob, have you ever seen a cigar box?" (You had to be there but "box" was used as a verb in this case.) And the best one, knowing that Nana was a wonderful baker, is this one:

> Pop: Rob, what's the best thing to put into a pie?
>
> Me: I don't know Pop, what is the best thing to put into a pie?
>
> Pop: Your teeth!

I am so thankful that Diane saved these letters. I hope and pray that as you read about his life, you got a glimpse into the heart of this wonderful man. The letters in this treasure box gave me a clearer picture of just how amazing he was. And his life continues to bless and guide me today.

The LORD is my rock, my fortress and my deliverer; my God is my rock, in whom I take refuge, my shield and the horn of my salvation, my stronghold.
Psalm 18:2

My Letter to Pop, Nana, and Uncle Fred

Dear Pop, Nana, and Uncle Fred,

How could I ever thank you for the letters you wrote and the legacy you left me?

Your faith and Godly example planted seeds in my younger years, even when I didn't realize it. And I believe that what you planted and watered has bloomed and continues to bless me and many others in my family. I am eternally grateful for the treasures you left me.

I will never forget the visits to your home in New Jersey, too many to count. The meals, the iced tea, the garden. I remember during my college years, whenever I would stop by, you would drop what you were doing and give me your full attention. I recall the conversations we had in the living room; Pop and Nana sat in their chairs and you insisted that I take the couch for myself. Uncle Fred pulled up a dining room chair and we talked.

Pop, you wrote most of the letters but I know that Nana and Uncle Fred were right there with you, cheering me on. You were in my first book and this book, and you'll be in the next one as well. That is a testament to the influence you continue to have in my life.

I miss you but can't wait to see you all again!!

Your loving and grateful grandson,

Rob

Here are a few excerpts from the many letters Pop wrote to me.

This first one was written right after our surprise visit to New Jersey during Thanksgiving, 1983. Pop always numbered his pages with Roman numerals. Here he was discussing his amazing garden.

The next shows how Pop often wrote the temperature at the top of his letters. And the last is one of Pop's shell boxes.

II

We do have a wonderful garden this year, the results of keeping it watered. Nona makes stewed tomatoes with onion and puts it over meal shape and it is delicious especially with your favorite ice tea. We hate to think what our electric and gas and water bill will be this month, everybodys for that matter

99 degrees Hot.

Chapter 7: Letter to Diane

A wife of noble character who can find?
She is worth far more than rubies.

Proverbs 31:10

WITHIN MY TREASURE CHEST, I ALSO FOUND A MOST CHERISHED NOTE FROM MY WIFE. It was the letter Diane wrote when I retired from my first career in 2016. It was part of a large book that she compiled based on letters from many employees, colleagues, and friends. At the time, I had no idea that she was preparing that book but it has become a keepsake I will cherish forever. I've included her letter at the end of this short chapter.

We didn't exchange many letters over the almost four-decades of marriage so far, but I do remember we passed notes to each other in class when we started dating in 1983. We have also given cards to each other over the years, each taking the time to write romantic notes inside. But surely, this book wouldn't be what it is without her, nor complete without my writing to her, in return.

My Letter to My Wife

Dear Diane,

A short note is insufficient to express the love, friendship, companionship, joy, and a million other words I could use to describe the blessing of being married to you.

I want to point out one of the sweetest things you ever did for me. That was the letter you wrote to me when I retired from my first career in 2016. With the long hours I spent in the office, a more than two-hour commute (on a good day), and numerous business trips all over the world, you took care of business at home. You never complained and always supported me. There is no earthly way that I could have made it without you.

You are the best spouse that God could have given me and I don't deserve you. You also are the best mother to our three wonderful daughters. And your life and influence have brought me closer to Jesus Christ.

A letter could not contain the words I need to describe how much I love you and how grateful I am that God made you my life partner on this journey. I can't imagine life without you.

With all my love forever,

Bob

To my Dearest Husband:

It was a white 3 X 5 note card that changed my life forever. On that spring day, I visited my college placement office looking for any job announcements that were recently posted. After graduating the previous spring this was a common routine for me; but this day was different. Hanging on the office bulletin board was a card with a hand written message: Jobs...3.5GPA...Call ###.

After a phone call, an application, an interview and another phone call, I was on the way to _____ Texas to start my career. Little did I know that I was about to meet my soul mate, my best friend and the greatest guy I ever knew. (I know this is where you would say: "but then you meet me instead". See, I know how you think. Hence, my soul mate.)

And so it was, July 25, 1983; we meet on the first day of class. Our first conversation was about New Jersey and the shore. Later that day we ate lunch together. I think it was when you bit into your catfish platter and meowed, I knew this was gonna be fun!

Yes, we had our first date, then more dates, engagement, move to NJ, marriage, first house, first child, move to PA, second child and third child. We had holidays, vacations, concerts, plays, sporting events and church. It really has been fun and we have many wonderful memories. There is however, another part of our lives that we sometimes fail to reflect on: your career.

Your _____ service was almost like music playing in the background during the movie of our life. It was always there but sometimes we took it for granted. Like your other amazing musical talents, you played this concert (work) like a gifted conductor. (Yes, now I know you are thinking of Seinfeld. Hence, soul mate.)

Over the years, your career has brought many wonderful people into your life and ours. It has also allowed you to travel the world and experience new things and share your experiences with us. But the bottom line, of course, is that it has provided an income that has allowed us to live comfortably, maintain a nice home and raise three wonderful children.

Despite your long commute, early hours and long days, you have always been there for your family and are a wonderful husband and father. You have also established yourself as an exemplary employee and a successful and respected supervisor. Again, as a conductor, you have been able to use your instruments (employees) to produce many wonderful musical pieces. (Is this music analogy getting totally tacky now?)

There was a lot of stress and frustration in being a supervisor, especially because you took your responsibilities so seriously. Sure there have been sour notes, skipped beats, pauses and verses that did not rhyme, but the audience has always benefitted from your hard work. Over the years, employees have come and gone, but I bet each one still remembers the tune they learned under your direction. I know that many of them are sad to see you exit the stage.

So, here it is 30 years later and you are retiring. This musical piece is coming to an end and it is both exciting and scary time in our lives. A lot of prayers and planning has gone into this difficult decision. There will be many changes in our lives and routines but we will trust in God's plan for us. But despite this song ending, there is one thing of which I am certain—the music will go on and it will continue to sound beautiful. And it will start with another note.

Thank you for the music you have brought into my life.

Love Always,

Diane

Chapter 8: Letter to Samantha

*Children are a heritage from the Lord,
offspring a reward from Him.*

Psalm 127:3

Among the retirement letters, I found a cherished note from my oldest daughter, Samantha. Sam enjoyed the benefits of being an only child for the first five years of her life. She paved the way for her two younger sisters academically, musically, athletically, and spiritually. She is a born leader and followed in my footsteps in terms of career path.

I am so grateful that the Lord gave me Sam as a daughter. Life is richer because of her and I couldn't be prouder of the woman and wife (to her wonderful husband Jeff) that she has become. The following letter doesn't come close to expressing the depth of my love and gratitude for her.

My Letter to Samantha

Dear Sam,

I will never forget the day you were born at a small hospital in central New Jersey. Mom and I were so young. I was in the delivery room and watched the miracle of your birth, and I cried tears of joy. I remember that they placed a knitted cap on your head and wrapped you in tin foil to keep you warm. I wasn't sure if we just had a baby or a baked potato!

You were and are our first. You came with no instruction manual so Mom and I were so careful with everything we did when you were little. I was away on business quite a bit during your high school years, but somehow, I managed to be there for your significant events.

I remember in high school when you juggled a difficult academic schedule, band, and cross-country. I tried to discourage you from having such a full plate but you embraced the joys of your activities, and you did each with excellence. Now you have a successful career and marriage. I am so proud of the woman you have become.

My prayer for you and our dear son-in-law is that you both continue to do your best and keep Jesus first in your marriage and your life.

With all of my love,

Dad

This is the letter Sam wrote for my first retirement:

> Dad,
>
> I bet you never thought this day would come, but here we are at your retirement! I don't know where to start other than saying it has been quite a crazy and busy year, but I'm glad I could be here to share this moment with you. This year has been memorable for our family: Laurie's graduation and move, your retirement, my wedding, etc. I have enjoyed the time we have gotten to spend together as a family and I have a greater appreciation for both our family and you, as leader of it.
>
> You have taught me so much over the years, including wisdom, kindness and a love for others. I never thought in a million years that I would be following in your career footsteps, but 7 years later here I am. I can only hope that 30 years down the road when I am standing where you are right now that I can look back and say I was loved and respected as a boss and coworker in the way that you are.
>
> No matter what you do after this, you have made a positive impact it so many lives, including mine, and you should look back and reflect on what an amazing thing that is!!! Happy Retirement Day! I love you!
>
> Your Daughter,
> Samantha

Chapter 9: Letter to Laurel

Then Esau looked up and saw the women and children. "Who are these with you?" he asked. Jacob answered, "They are the children God has graciously given your servant."

Genesis 33:5

ANOTHER TREASURE IN THE BOX WAS A LETTER FROM MY SECOND DAUGHTER, LAUREL. My middle daughter Laurel (or "Laurie" as we still refer to her) was definitely on the shy side growing up. Today, she is outgoing, gregarious, and adventurous, the antithesis of her personality when she was young. Her metamorphosis taught me that we should never label or pigeonhole children when they are young. They are a precious gift from God. As in my own life, I am not who

I was. When I look at each of my girls today, it amazes me how unique and gifted they are. They have different personalities and tastes but have common interests. I am so grateful that they get along so well.

Laur could not attend my retirement luncheon because she had just finished graduate school and started a new job in Boston. But her letter touched me deeply. My letter to her is an inadequate attempt to express my love and gratitude for her.

My Letter to Laurel

Dear Laur,

I vividly remember the day you were born. We had enjoyed Thanksgiving dinner earlier that day and Mom went into labor that night. Once Mom was admitted, it wasn't too long before you came into this world. I was scared because there were issues when you were born in the middle of the night, and our pediatrician was called in to assist. I am so grateful that you were healthy.

You were sensitive and shy as a child, even up through your teen years. It's hard to believe how adventurous you've become. You orchestrated your own college semester abroad in Australia and you've hiked, camped, rock climbed, and run all over the world. You also gave me a passion to hike and spend some time in the woods!

I am so proud of you and grateful for the woman you've become. You perform excellently in your career and excel at everything you endeavor.

I pray that you continue to do your best and keep Jesus first in your life.

With all of my love,

Dad

This is the letter Laurie wrote for my first retirement:

> Dad,
>
> I can't believe you're retiring! Your work has been such a huge part of your life and I know it meant a lot to you. You had the opportunity to meet so many great people and travel to amazing places. I will never forget when you took us to Utah to show us a bit of your world, and to Hawaii while you were there on business for three amazing weeks when we were younger. I am so excited for whatever your next step in life is. Thank you for always inspiring me. ☺
>
> Love,
>
> Laurie

Chapter 10: Letter to Hayley

Start children off on the way they should go, and even when they are old they will not turn from it.

Proverbs 22:6

MY THIRD DAUGHTER ALSO WROTE ME A PRECIOUS LETTER AFTER MY FIRST RETIREMENT. Hayley, our baby, just turned twenty-six, which is a reminder of how quickly time goes by. She has never liked the limelight nor being the center of attention. But greatness and success seem to find people who humbly, quietly, and intentionally do the right thing. Hayley is a compassionate young lady of integrity with unique gifts, like her older sisters. Her sense of humor and cheerful spirit are infectious. This letter to her is insufficient to express my love and appreciation for her.

My Letter to My Third Daughter, Hayley

Dear Hayley,

I was getting ready for a business trip to California on the day Mom announced that she was pregnant with you. On the flight to Sacramento the next day you were all I could think about. Sam would be almost nine years old and Laurie almost four when you were born.

I remember the day of your birth like it was yesterday. We almost didn't make it to the hospital because I kept reassuring Mom that she "had plenty of time." You were born first thing in the morning and your sisters couldn't wait to come to the hospital and hold you.

All through your childhood, college years, and now in adulthood, you have always been a person of integrity, humility, and hard work. You never call attention to yourself and quietly love and serve others, in your life and career. You would literally give the shirt off of your back to help people and that is a Godly trait.

I love you and am so grateful for who you are and the woman you've become.

I pray that you continue to do your best and keep Jesus first in your life.

With all of my love,

Dad

This is the letter Hayley wrote for my first retirement:

Dad,

I want to first off wish you a huge congratulations on your retirement. It's still incredible to me that you have been working　　　　　since long before I was born. You were truly blessed throughout all those years with all sorts of friendships and memories to keep with you. I want to thank you for setting an example of what working hard and persevering looks like. I also want to thank you for not only being a good boss but for being a good father as well. You've always made sure you were very involved in my, Laurie's, and Sam's lives both throughout our childhoods as well as now. Despite working, which I understand can make it difficult at times to balance everything, you always made sure you tried your best to make it to school functions such as sporting events, band/chorus concerts, etc., and for that I am very grateful. I also remember you sending little gifts from work travels and different places you've been to which are memories I will keep with me and cherish. As you retire, enjoy every moment life has to offer. Like you always say, every day is a blessing, so enjoy it! I love you and wish you a very happy retirement!

- Hayley

Chapter 11: Treasures in Heaven

The kingdom of heaven is like treasure hidden in a field. When a man found it, he hid it again, and then in his joy went and sold all he had and bought that field. Again, the kingdom of heaven is like a merchant looking for fine pearls. When he found one of great value, he went away and sold everything he had and bought it.

Matthew 13:44 – 46

IN THIS BOOK, I'VE SPOKEN A GREAT DEAL ABOUT TREASURE. The word "treasure" has several meanings. I've heard it defined as "stored up or hoarded wealth." In this book I want to camp on another definition I heard which referenced "something of great worth or value." The letters I rediscovered in the decorative box are indeed now one of my greatest treasures. In fact, I believe that the words in these letters are treasures which are stored up in heaven.

You may be thinking, "Okay Bob, I thought that this book was about letters and the great stories you discovered." Well, that's part of it. But I go back to the opening verse in the Introduction of this book:

Since, then, you have been raised with Christ, set your hearts on things above, where Christ is, seated at the right hand of God. Set your minds on things above, not on earthly things. For you died, and your life is now hidden with Christ in God.
Colossians 3:1-3

You see my friend, the letters, the stories, and the family memories, would mean little to me apart from the One who has blessed me with my very life. In fact, without Jesus Christ as the center of my life, I may never have discovered these hidden treasures and experienced the blessings I've shared with you. I didn't fully appreciate the words spoken into my life back then. In fact, I remembered very little about the contents of these letters as I read through them now. But God used Pop, Nana, my mom and dad, Diane's mom and dad, Uncle Fred, Grandmom, and a host of others to plant and water seeds in my life.

These letters encouraged me during the times when I questioned everything and they encourage me still. I believe that God, through His Holy Spirit, used people, over a long period of time, to draw me to Himself, and fully bloom the seeds that were planted long ago. Ultimately, I made the decision to surrender my life to Him in the early 1990s. Please understand that I did nothing to earn or deserve His amazing love and grace. He paid it all and gets all of the glory.

As I finished reading through the letters in the decorative box, I realized that they are genuine treasures which have been stored in heaven. With the words of love and encouragement contained therein, I believe that Mom, Dad, Pop and other family members, inspired by their love for God, accumulated treasures for eternity. Their words are already reaping dividends for my generation and I believe will transcend this life.

You may be saying, "Bob, what in the world are you talking about? How can we store up treasures in heaven?" I take you back to the passage from Matthew 6:19-21 which I referred to in Chapter 1 of this book. Here it is once more:

Do not store up for yourselves treasures on earth, where moths and vermin destroy, and where thieves break in and steal. But store up for yourselves treasures in heaven, where moths and vermin do not destroy, and where thieves do not break in and steal. For where your treasure is, there your heart will be also.

Notice how the passage ends, "Where your treasure is, there your heart will be also." It all boils down to priorities. Where is my affection, attention, and attitude focused? What is most important to me? What is important to you, honestly?

Let me ask you a question, one I've asked myself repeatedly: What in your life holds the greatest worth or value? Perhaps you've never consciously thought about it. Is it money, some possession, a person, or maybe something intangible such as your career title? I've left space for you to jot down an item or two after you've pondered this question. Be honest!

My greatest treasures are:

_____

_____

If I'm being totally honest, for the longest time my greatest treasures consisted of things which do not last, e.g., my career, how much money I made, and the need to be significant. In summary, my treasures were wrapped up in "self." My very identity was tied up in those things for a long time. Don't get me wrong, I loved my wife and children and would give my life for any of them (this is still true today). But in my heart, the things I placed my hope in were all about "me." And I still struggle with perfectionism. I need the Lord's help daily to keep things in perspective. Striving to be like Jesus, in the power of the Holy Spirit, is a wonderful way to live. He calls us to a holy (set apart) life and provides all we need to live it. In contrast, perfectionism can cause stress, burnout, and other health issues. I speak from experience. Again, being totally transparent with you, even today I need to guard against elevating temporary things to the detriment of the eternal things that really matter. I need God's help to do that.

You've likely heard the saying, "You can't take it with you." This statement hit home recently as I lost several relatives and friends over the past year. A dear neighbor who went home to be with the Lord in 2020 quoted a similar saying which went something like, "You never see a U-Haul at funeral." It's true, our earthly treasures are staying here. My home, cars, bank account, clothes, guitars, saxophones, and anything else I can touch will not be coming with me. In fact, they'll belong to someone else. Also, the accomplishments in my career and any other accolades will eventually be forgotten. Now that may sound a little depressing but there is good news: I believe that there actually are some things that you and I *can* take with us. It's not what you may be thinking. There are treasures we can store up in heaven, right now!

Let me caveat what I'm about to say with the statement that I am not a theologian or Bible scholar. But I believe that these words of Jesus are plain enough for anyone to understand. I think what He is saying is this: The things of this world, including wealth, status, accolades, and creature comforts, are not lasting. They can and will deteriorate or be taken away from us. It is good to enjoy what God has generously provided for us but foolish to put our faith in these things. More importantly, fixation on earthly treasures can distract us from what truly matters which is our love for God and relationship with Him. And the fruit of that relationship carries over to our love and service for family and our fellow human beings.

If you jump down to verse 24 in Matthew it says this:

No one can serve two masters. Either you will hate the one and love the other, or you will be devoted to the one and despise the other. You cannot serve both God and money.

The question I have to continually ask myself is: Am I serving God or has something else taken a higher priority in my life? How about you?

Thanks be to God, I believe Jesus is saying that there *are* things which last beyond this life, things that have eternal value. Our love and gratitude for God, in response to all He has done for me and all of humankind, are treasures which can be stored up in heaven. Our love and service for others, in response to our love for the Lord, is another treasure which can be stored up for eternity. The godly legacy we leave behind can be an eternal treasure, blessing future generations in our families.

In Deuteronomy 11:18-20 it says this:

> *Fix these words of mine in your hearts and minds; tie them as symbols on your hands and bind them on your foreheads. Teach them to your children, talking about them when you sit at home and when you walk along the road, when you lie down and when you get up. Write them on the doorframes of your houses and on your gates, so that your days and the days of your children may be many in the land the Lord swore to give your ancestors, as many as the days that the heavens are above the earth.*

The Book of Deuteronomy was written specifically to the nation of Israel but I believe that the lessons are applicable for us all. In fact, verses from Deuteronomy are referred to in the New Testament more than any other Old Testament books with the exception of the Psalms and Isaiah. The purpose of the foregoing passage, in my opinion, is to articulate the need to internalize God's Word, apply it to our own lives, and to pass it on to future generations. Imagine the impact to our world if we were diligent about this as totally-committed followers of Jesus Christ. Have I done this with my own children and those I encounter? Am I doing it now?

As I read these letters in the treasure box, I realized that my family, Pop and my mom especially, invested heavily in my spiritual life, and they may not have been aware of that. I can't imagine where I would be if those seeds had not been planted. Whether they realized it or not, they were laying up treasures in heaven which will last for eternity! I pray that I can store up similar treasures which will last beyond this short life here on earth. My book here has been one small attempt to do that.

In the Gospel of Luke 12, verses 19-21, Jesus makes the point that our affections can be focused in the wrong place:

And he told them this parable: "The ground of a certain rich man yielded an abundant harvest. He thought to himself, 'What shall I do? I have no place to store my crops.' Then he said, 'This is what I'll do. I will tear down my barns and build bigger ones, and there I will store my surplus grain. And I'll say to myself, 'You have plenty of grain laid up for many years. Take life easy; eat, drink and be merry.' But God said to him, 'You fool! This very night your life will be demanded from you. Then who will get what you have prepared for yourself?' This is how it will be with whoever stores up things for themselves but is not rich toward God."

My friend, there is nothing wrong with material wealth. God gives us all things to enjoy (1 Timothy 6:17). James 1:17 says,

Every good and perfect gift is from above, coming down from the Father of the heavenly lights, who does not change like shifting shadows.

If you consider the standard of living and income level in this country, compared to most others in the world, we are extremely blessed. Yes, there are issues, but we (myself included) sometimes can complain about what we don't have rather than the blessings we do have. The reality is that we have abundance beyond belief. And God calls us to be good stewards of what He has provided, no matter how insignificant we may think it is. When we give and invest in others, God blesses it. However, we can also become obsessed with wealth and material "stuff" to the point that we forget about Who provides it for us (Ecclesiastes 5:19).

Throughout the Bible we are taught to love and serve others, to forgive, to be generous, and to be grateful. It all comes down to the priorities and affections of our hearts. Again, imagine if professing Christians lived this way and pushed secondary issues to a lower priority. When Jesus was asked what is the greatest commandment, He answered this way:

Love the Lord your God all your heart and with all your soul and with all your mind and with all your strength and love your neighbor as yourself.
Mark 12:30-31

These treasures I speak of are not born out of religion but rather a relationship with the living God through Jesus Christ based on His love, grace, mercy, and goodness. When we love and put Him first on our priority list, and we love our "neighbor" which excludes no one, we store up treasures in heaven. A person's heart belongs to whatever it "treasures."

Since I have been raised with Christ to new life, He calls me to set my heart and mind on the eternal things, not on earthly things. Only the treasures I store up in heaven will last. For me, a big part of that calling is sharing the love of Jesus Christ with everyone I meet.

Here's one other thing I discovered as I explored the contents of my treasure box: As wonderful as the letters are, as much as I do believe that these are treasures which are being stored up in heaven, there is one thing greater: God's Holy Word, the Bible. In it I have discovered the life-changing, transforming, one-of-a-kind, inestimable, valuable treasure that I can hold in my hand. No, I can't take my physical Bible with me when God calls me home, but the treasures inside, His very words, are certainly coming along (Matt 24:35). This treasure is eternal and points to the only One who can rescue us from this sinful world and give us eternal life: Jesus Christ, my Lord and Savior.

As we come to the end of this book, I encourage you to seek the Lord first and fix your eyes on Jesus Christ. Enjoy what you have but don't put your faith in stuff or anything else that takes the place of Jesus. It took me years to understand that this worldview doesn't work. Like I did for so long, you may think it's working when things are going well but it doesn't take much to bring us to rock bottom. Our money, our career, our status, our health, you name it, can all be taken in an instant. Then where do we place our faith and hope?

I encourage you to take the time to build a legacy by sharing your heart with someone who needs a word of hope. Maybe this involves a phone call, a letter (a text or e-mail works too), or just reaching out to a neighbor in need. Ask God to open your heart and bring someone into your path who needs encouragement. Offer to pray for them. You'll be amazed at the opportunities God will bring your way. I can't tell you what that will look like for you but you'll be astounded at what God will do and you will be laying up treasures in heaven. These are the things that last and have eternal value!

My goal is that they may be encouraged in heart and united in love, so that they may have the full riches of complete understanding, in order that they may know the mystery of God, namely, Christ, in whom are hidden all the treasures of wisdom and knowledge.

Colossians 2:2-3

Chapter 12: Bob's Letter to You

But our citizenship is in heaven. And we eagerly await a Savior from there, the LORD Jesus Christ...

Philippians 3:20

Dear Friend, please accept my sincere appreciation for taking the time to read this book and allowing me to give you a glimpse into my family and my heart. I truly pray that you've been blessed by the letters and stories from the treasures I discovered in this little box. I want to take a few minutes and share some final thoughts with you.

First, let me sincerely ask, "how are you doing?" I mean, how are you *really* doing? If you're anything like me, your automatic response, your first thought, might be, "Fine, or great!" And the conversation usually ends there.

But often times, we are not "fine." Personally, I'm not naturally the type of person who likes to open up my life to others and share the struggles and weaknesses I am experiencing. Perhaps you can relate? Many of us, myself included, want to give the appearance that we have it all together. I can really put on a good front and make it appear that life is all sunshine, lollipops, and rainbows. But if I'm being totally transparent with you, many times, I don't have it all together and I need help. I also need hope. How about you?

It doesn't take much for us to get discouraged these days when we look at the condition of our world and the circumstances in our lives. The negatives are not that hard to find and can consume our perspective. Of course, there is nothing new under the sun but recent events have shined a spotlight on those things that aren't right in our world. Moreover, the internet, 24/7 news, and bombardment of information can overwhelm us. We can get to the point where we become cynical, negative, or hopeless. Where do we go to find truth? How about hope? What about help? To whom or what can we turn?

I am not aware of anyone who cannot use some hope right now. When I think about the word "hope," my mind goes to expressions such as, "I hope that this car repair is not expensive" or, "I hope that it doesn't rain on our vacation." In this regard, "hope" is a desire we have for something to occur. It's not a certainty, but more of a wish. In the Bible the idea of hope is tied to faith, a confidence we have based on God's sure promises. The words used for "hope" in the original Biblical languages indicate a certainty, a confident expectation. Hebrews 11:1 says,

> *Now faith is confidence in what we hope for and assurance about what we do not see.*

We take hold of this hope by fixing our eyes on Jesus, setting our hearts and minds on things above, and laying up treasures in heaven. This involves focusing on the Upper Story even when it seems like things are falling apart in our Lower Story. My pastor often quotes the last part of 2 Chronicles 20:12 which says, *"We do not know what to do, but our eyes are on You."* Jesus is our hope, our help, and the One to Whom we can turn in good times and in bad.

If you are a true believer, one who has put your complete faith in Jesus Christ and His finished work on the Cross for your salvation, let me remind you that this world is not our home. The Bible says that we are pilgrims (sojourners) here and that our true citizenship is in heaven (1 Peter 2:11, Philippians 3:20). We are in this world to love and serve God, and to love and serve people, but we are not to be *of* this world (John 15:12, John 17:14-16).

Based on the promises in the Bible, God's inerrant Word and love letter to us, we have the certainty of His forgiveness, presence, wisdom, guidance, and abundant eternal life which begins the moment we commit our lives to Him. That, my friend, is an unfathomable hope beyond what I deserve. Hebrews 6:19-20 sums up the matter:

We have this hope as an anchor for the soul, firm and secure. It enters the inner sanctuary behind the curtain, where our forerunner, Jesus, has entered on our behalf.

The hope the writer refers to is found in the previous verse (18):

God did this so that, by two unchangeable things in which it is impossible for God to lie, we who have fled to take hold of the hope set before us may be greatly encouraged.

My friend, I have told lies and so have you. Big ones and little ones, and ones that distort the truth just a little. But thanks be to God, He doesn't lie. He cannot. It is not in His nature. Therefore, every promise He has made is true and we can depend on them if we are truly His children. His promises give us the hope that is rock-solid, firm and secure!

God is also our "help" in all times and circumstances. Psalm 121:1 - 3 says,

I lift up my eyes to the mountains— where does my help come from? My help comes from the LORD, the Maker of heaven and earth.

Here is an amazing truth which gives me great comfort: God Himself, in the Person of the Holy Spirit, lives inside of me. My friend, if you have given your life to Jesus Christ, God Himself actually lives in you as well! The Holy Spirit is God's presence living in the believer! What an awesome truth—beyond my simple comprehension!

The Bible has so much to say about how the Holy Spirit gives us wisdom, guidance, comfort, help, and so much more. I'll share just a couple of verses with you:

Don't you know that you yourselves are God's temple and that God's Spirit dwells in your midst?
1 Corinthians 3:16

Do you not know that your bodies are temples of the Holy Spirit, who is in you, whom you have received from God? You are not your own...
1 Corinthians 6:19

I encourage you to do a personal study of the Holy Spirit in God's Word. It will bless you immensely! If God

Himself lives inside of us when we receive His free gift of salvation, it says something about how precious you and I are to Him! We have everything we need in Him. This is confirmed in my Nana's favorite verse from Philippians 4:13 which I shared earlier, "I can do all things in Him who strengthens me."

Even if the world seems to be unravelling before our eyes, God is working in ways we cannot see. We can trust Him and His sure promises. Hebrews 13:8 says, "Jesus Christ is the same yesterday and today and forever." Thank God for that truth! I have let people down in my life and people have also let me down. Not so with Jesus. He is the friend who sticks closer than a brother. In the times in which we live, it is so comforting to know that there is a God we can depend on, always, no matter what!

Let me close this letter with two points:

First, you may have noticed that I've written quite a bit in this book about "treasures," those things that are valuable to us. Spending time journaling and writing books has helped me to dig even deeper into the Bible, God's love letter to humanity.

As I write this, I'm thinking about how it all started on the day Jesus rescued me in the early 1990s. In a very real sense, you and I are His treasures, precious souls whom He loves and would do anything for. In fact, He did *everything* by loving us enough to come into this world and die for our sins.

It still amazes me how patient He was and how He never stopped loving and pursuing me, even when I kept saying "no, I'll live life my own way." He could have taken me out when I was living in rebellion and I would have been eternally lost. But God showed me grace, mercy, and compassion. I love this parable Jesus tells in Matthew 18:12-14:

What do you think? If a man owns a hundred sheep, and one of them wanders away, will he not leave the ninety-nine on the hills and go to look for the one that wandered off? And if he finds it, truly I tell you, he is happier about that one sheep than about the ninety-nine that did not wander off. In the same way your Father in heaven is not willing that any of these little ones should perish.

This reminds me of a short story from my childhood. When I was a little boy, I had a miniature collie named, "Twiggy." We obtained her from an elderly neighbor who lived two doors down from us. He and his wife could no longer care for the young dog and offered her to us. My first dog, "Bingo," had been killed by a car. My parents didn't tell me until I was older; for years I thought that he had just run away. But after Bingo, I really wanted another dog. Thankfully, after I pleaded with him, Dad agreed.

Twiggy was a wonderful dog and companion, but she had one major flaw: She did not like thunderstorms and was inconsolable when they occurred. Whenever a bad storm rolled in, she would panic and pace around the house, scared, and panting rapidly. I always felt badly because nothing I could do would comfort her.

On one occasion, Twiggy was out in the yard when a big storm hit. By the time we opened the back door to retrieve her, she had vanished. I was devastated and incredulous that she would survive. We had a busy street behind us, an interstate two blocks away, and hundreds of other ways she could meet her demise. I was heartbroken. We searched everywhere and spread the word by talking to neighbors and erecting posters with a reward for her return.

A week passed with no sign of her. Deep down I was losing hope but wouldn't give up until we found her, one way or the other. By the second week I figured she was gone forever, perhaps dead in the woods or lying on a road somewhere. But I wouldn't stop searching, even though my hope was just a sliver. Then a miracle happened. It had been two weeks but a neighbor spotted her in the next town over, by the factory where he worked, and coaxed her home. We had no idea how she survived, where she had been for two weeks, or who may have helped her. It didn't matter; my dog, my best friend was home and I rejoiced. She was a lost treasure but now she had been found.

Twiggy remained by my side and was always full of kisses for me. She lived a great, long life and it wasn't until I was in college that her health started to fail. I was home one weekend and had to say goodbye to her. Twiggy had gotten to the point where she was suffering and Dad would have her put down that week. It was so hard and I'm choked up remembering that after all of these years. Pets are family and you know exactly what I'm talking about if you've ever had and lost any. I loved that little dog.

My friend, Jesus came to this earth because we are valuable to Him. He loves us and won't give up pursuing us until we "come home." Luke 19:10 says:

For the Son of Man came to seek and to save the lost.

Luke 15:7 says:

I tell you that in the same way there will be more rejoicing in heaven over one sinner who repents than over ninety-nine righteous persons who do not need to repent.

Have you taken hold of this treasure for yourself?

Here's the second and final point: There is an urgency to get right with God before it is too late. I also don't want anyone to stand before the Lord and say, "Bob, you were my friend and knew this but never told me about the love of God and the need to be saved from our sins."

My dear friend, I love you too much to keep this truth from you. John 3:18 says,

Whoever believes in him is not condemned, but whoever does not believe stands condemned already because they have not believed in the name of God's one and only Son.

Romans 10:9 tells us*:*

If you declare with your mouth, "Jesus is Lord," and believe in your heart that God raised him from the dead, you will be saved.

If you have not given your life to Christ, can I lovingly ask you to consider that *right now*? There will come a day, through death or the return of Jesus, where we all will give an account for how we lived. If we are depending on our own "righteousness" we will face God's judgment and be eternally lost. Isaiah 64:6 says:

All of us have become like one who is unclean, and all our righteous acts are like filthy rags; we all shrivel up like a leaf, and like the wind our sins sweep us away.

If you wait until tomorrow, or even one more minute, it may be too late.

James 4:13-14 tells us:

Now listen, you who say, "Today or tomorrow we will go to this or that city, spend a year there, carry on business and make money." Why, you do not even know what will happen tomorrow. What is your life? You are a mist that appears for a little while and then vanishes.

True belief entails placing your trust in the finished work of Jesus Christ for the forgiveness of your sins. John 14:6 makes it clear:

Jesus answered, "I am the way and the truth and the life. No one comes to the Father except through me."

In 1st Corinthians 15:3 – 4, the apostle Paul gets to the heart of the matter:

For what I received I passed on to you as of first importance: that Christ died for our sins according to the Scriptures, that He was buried, that He was raised on the third day according to the Scriptures...

This last story is the best way I can think of to illustrate our lost condition and the absolute need to be rescued while there is still time.

I told you all about my dear grandfather Pop and the influence he had, and still has, on my journey. When I was younger, Pop was working in his house when he heard the desperate cries of a neighbor in distress. As he looked out his front door, he was horrified to see that the house across the street was fully engulfed in flames. He looked up and saw a young girl at a second story window, trapped by the flames and smoke from the first floor. Her parents were away and she was helpless to save herself. Her choices were to jump or hope that the fire and smoke would not consume her. Either way, she was doomed in that condition. She needed someone to rescue her immediately.

Pop thought nothing of his own safety but grabbed a tall ladder from under the porch and quickly made his way across the street. He propped the ladder against the burning house and provided the only way to life for that little girl. As Pop climbed the ladder and reached out his arms, she grabbed onto him and he and carried her down to safety.

This precious girl was in a helpless situation. She could have chosen to hide or refuse Pop's rescue; in which case she would have been tragically lost. But she chose to trust her rescuer who provided the only way to life. Pop did everything possible for her to be rescued but she had to accept the only solution which existed. The house was gutted and the family was able to rebuild. But that girl who is God's precious Creation, whose life could have ended that day, had new life.

My friend, that is a crude metaphor for what God did for each of us, but it illustrates our condition. We are helpless and lost apart from Jesus Christ and there is nothing we can do to be righteous before a holy God. I'll let the Bible speak for itself. Ephesians 2: 2 – 3 says,

As for you, you were dead in your transgressions and sins, in which you used to live when you followed the ways of this world and of the ruler of the kingdom of the air, the spirit who is now at work in those who are disobedient. All of us also lived among them at one time, gratifying the cravings of our flesh and following its desires and thoughts. Like the rest, we were by nature deserving of wrath.

But here is the great news from Ephesians 2:4 -10:

But because of His great love for us, God, who is rich in mercy, made us alive with Christ even when we were dead in transgressions—it is by grace you have been saved. And God raised us up with Christ and seated us with Him in the heavenly realms in Christ Jesus, in order that in the coming ages He might show the incomparable riches of His grace, expressed in His kindness to us in Christ Jesus. For it is by grace you have been saved, through faith—and this is not from yourselves, it is the gift of God— not by works, so that no one can boast.

When we say "yes" to Jesus's invitation, we spend our lives loving, serving, and growing in our relationship with Him. We owe Him everything! He is our Savior, Redeemer, our Lord, our very life. He is Jesus, our Almighty Companion. To Him be all praise, honor, and glory!

Jesus loves you, my friend, more than anyone else ever could. Be encouraged and invest your life in loving and serving Him and everyone you encounter.

Let me say a word to those of us who claim to follow Jesus: Are we (am I) seeking Him, loving Him, and living according to His Word, not the ways of this world? Do the words we say reflect the fact that we are His ambassadors and bear the image of Jesus Christ to a watching world? Am I more concerned about being "right" or pushing my own agenda than being Jesus to someone? Am I grateful? Are we looking for opportunities to share the Gospel, the good news of Jesus Christ as our Lord and Savior, with everyone we encounter? Are we (am I) doing this in a loving, not overbearing way, under the influence of the Holy Spirit? The Bible says this in 1 Peter 3:15:

> *But in your hearts revere Christ as LORD. Always be prepared to give an answer to everyone who asks you to give the reason for the hope that you have. But do this with gentleness and respect...*

It's easy sometimes to forget the last part of that verse. We need to tell our story, under the inspiration of the Holy Spirit, but we do it in a sincere, loving way.

Why do I tell you all of this in a book about what I discovered in a treasure chest? It's really simple: Because of what Jesus Christ has done for me, I can do no less than tell my story. He totally transformed my life. I am eternally grateful for His gift of salvation, His love, presence, patience, mercy, wisdom, provision, and I could go on and on.

Friend, I am no one special, average at best. I'm just telling you that I was a lost soul and Jesus gave me life.

You may have many reasons for rejecting Jesus Christ (I've been there myself) but I beg you to look at Him, His life, and what He did for you. The overwhelming evidence is there. You just need to believe and place your complete trust in Him. I am only saved by the grace of God. Apart from Jesus Christ I can do nothing, and His love and faithfulness give me reason to live and to love and serve others. There is nothing worthy or good in me. But in Jesus Christ, I am a new creation (2 Corinthians 5:17).

No matter where you are in this journey, I pray that God will reveal to you what it means to store up treasures in heaven. He has gifted each of us in some special way for service. Each morning I ask the Lord to bring someone across my path who needs encouragement. He has never failed to answer that simple prayer. Ask Him to help you use your gifts to bless and encourage others, for His glory!

A few years ago, just prior to Christmas, I had my Sunday School class do a little exercise. One-at-a-time, each person sat in a chair in the middle of the room. Consequently, each class member stated at least one thing that they appreciated about the person in the chair. The encouragement and blessings which came out of that exercise were amazing. No matter what we may think of ourselves, each of us is precious and gifted in some way. Many of us didn't see what those who observed us could see. And Jesus sees us even more clearly and loves us more than any person could.

Whether you are young or old, single, or married, whatever your situation, I encourage you to leave a godly legacy to your families, your children, and everyone God brings across your path. Ask the Lord for opportunities. Enjoy your loved ones while they are here. It sounds cliché but it's so true: the time goes by so quickly. Write the letter, make the call, spend time with them. This life is short and tomorrow is not guaranteed. You will be laying up for yourselves treasures in heaven, those things which will never fade away or perish...

I love you dear friend and I pray God's richest blessings upon your life.

Your friend in Christ,

Bob

He has caused his wonders to be remembered; the Lord is gracious and compassionate.
Psalm 111:4

Anxiety weighs down the heart, but a kind word cheers it up.
Proverbs 12:25

Yet to all who did receive him, to those who believed in his name, he gave the right to become children of God — children born not of natural descent, nor of human decision or a husband's will, but born of God.
John 1:12-13

About the Author

BOB JONES IS AN AVERAGE GUY FROM NEW JERSEY WHO IS ALSO THE AUTHOR OF "AVERAGE MAN, ALMIGHTY COMPANION." He is passionate about sharing the love of Jesus Christ with everyone he meets, through encouraging and often humorous stories. Bob is the father of three amazing grown daughters and lives in Central Pennsylvania with his wife of 36+ years. He enjoys music, hiking, reading, and of course, writing books and blogs. Connect with Bob online through his website **AverageManMessage.com.**

Additional copies of this book, as well as Bob's first release, *Average Man, Almighty Companion* are available at Amazon.com or BarnesandNoble.com.

Get one for the "average" guy in your life.

**Connect with Bob at
AverageManMessage.com**

Made in the USA
Monee, IL
10 September 2021